PLYMOUTH'S HISTORIC BARBICAN

CHRIS ROBINSON

CW00689309

British Library Cataloguing in Publication Data

A catalogue record for this book is available from the British Library

ISBN 978-0-9543480-5-2

Written by Chris Robinson
Design Chris Robinson & Ewan McKnight
© Chris Robinson 2007

First published 2007

All rights reserved. No part of this publication may be reproduced
stored in a retrieval system or transmitted, in any form or by any other means,
electronic, mechanical, photocopying, recording or otherwise
without the prior permission of Pen & Ink (Publishing).

Published by
Pen & Ink Publishing
34 New Street, Barbican
Plymouth PL1 2NA
Tel; 01752 705337/228120
Fax; 01752 770001
www.chrisrobinson.co.uk

Printed and bound in Great Britain by
Latimer Trend & Company Ltd
Estover Close
Plymouth PL6 7PL

Devon

CONTENTS

PETER STEDMAN

Born in Colebrook, Plympton, in 1920, Peter Stedman is a founder director of the Plymouth Barbican Association. During the Second World War he was in the heart of the action in some of the major events of the conflict: Dunkirk, El Alemein, Italy and the D-Day landing on the beaches of Normandy. After the war he established a fine reputation for himself as a partner with chartered surveyors Taylor Son & Creber and as a key director of the Sutton Harbour Company. Today he is the sole surviving continuously-serving director of the Barbican Association.

FOREWORD

In 1936 I was a teenager fresh out of Hoe Grammar School. I worked for an architect - William Roseveare. Slum clearance was taking place and one of my jobs was to survey properties listed as 'unfit for human habitation' and show on plans, where possible, how at small expense they could be made 'fit'. The difference between the two meant a considerable difference to the compensation paid. Sometimes at the end of the day I had to de-louse myself. It was a harsh introduction to the state of some of our older properties.

On September 5 1939, less than 48 hours after war had been declared, I volunteered for the army, taking the King's Shilling in Plymouth Museum. I was eighteen. Some 18 months later in May 1941, now a twenty-year-old second Lieutenant, I came home on embarkation leave to my parents who had moved from Plymouth to Tavistock. At Bedfore Square I boarded a Western National double-decker. I was disconcerted to hear conversations about the great damage to the Dockyard through bombing, and then I was surprised when the bus stopped at Sherwell and everyone got off. I walked past the Museum, the Library, the Harvest Home and through Drake's Circus and then came the shock. What had been Old Town Street was now a pathway through the rubble. I had seen similar scenes in Belgium and France, but this was my home town and the shock was awful.

After my release from the army in October 1945 I came back to Plymouth and spent six months, as directed, working for an architect, mainly drawing plans for in-fill houses in the gaps in terraces. Like so many of my contemporaries, with similar experiences, the war had made us grow up quickly and equipped us to shoulder responsibility beyond that which might be considered normal. It was a key element in bringing together a band of young men eager to get things done and who would join Round Table, the Junior Chamber of Commerce and some, in due course, the Barbican Association.

The City had been very far-sighted in getting Sir Patrick Abercrombie together with the City Engineer, Paton Watson to produce a Plan For Plymouth, while the war still raged. After it was over there were many grave problems to be tackled. Housing was urgently needed, the population having dropped by nearly half, a city centre had to be built, Plymouth was at the end of 'the longest lane in England': a bridge across the Tamar was needed and what about the slums that had not been blitzed?

A local solicitor, Ralph Luscombe, called a meeting attended by a dozen or so, and referred to a proposal that the City Council was considering to sweep away properties north of Citadel Road down to Sutton Harbour. It was decided to set up a committee to look into the matter and Jimmy Woodrow, of steel fabricators Blight & White, was elected chairman. We were determined to fight the Council and while we had much sympathy, and support, we lacked credibility … and money.

We all joined the old Plymouth Society but found it moribund and so we set up the Plymouth Barbican Association. One of the difficulties was that the Government offered subsidies towards the cost of a new council house for every property found to be 'unfit for human habitation'. We had two councillors, one from either side, Stanley Goodman and Leslie Paul, who were sympathetic and helpful. We found out that a house that was unfit need not be demolished as long as it was not used as living accommodation. The Council offered to lease to us for 999 years, six adjoining houses in New Street. We had to find guarantors for £100,000 … and we did.

Four stalwarts each pledged £25,000; Jimmy Woodrow, CP Brown of Brown, Wills and Nicholson, Humphrey Woolcombe, solicitor and descendant of Henry Woolcombe (who did so much for Plymouth at the beginning of the 19th century) and Gerald Whitmarsh, an accountant.

It was a very important moment. We were up and running. Now it was time to raise cash and save more properties with the support we were attracting. Our list of patrons read like something out of Burke's Peerage.

Since that time the Association has gone from strength to strength with a rent roll in excess of £150,000 a year. This is a lot of money but we have learnt that to pay for major repairs; to maintain the properties in as good condition as possible and keep abreast of modern legislation requires very careful management.

One incident I particularly remember occurred some twenty years ago. A number of us met on the top floor of one of the New Street properties to discuss some problem and several city officials were present. One, a senior planning official said to me almost as an aside: "I don't know why you do not use these storeys as flatlets." I said "because you people have always said we must not!" Thus planning principles can sometimes turn around with time. The planning officer was Vic French, now retired, one of our current directors.

I trust that this book will be of interest to those both present and future who have a feel for the Barbican and our lessons may be of help to others. This is the story of the first fifty years. We have recently set up the Plymouth Barbican Association South West Image Bank, in one of our Looe Street properties (No.32). This is to digitise and make accessible the collection of two million photographic negatives we saved from the Western Morning News and Evening Herald. There will be more to do

.

Peter Stedman – *October 2007*

ACKNOWLEDGEMENTS

This book would not have been written, nor would there have been much to write about, had it not been for the Plymouth Barbican Association Ltd. Formed fifty years ago to thwart local authority proposals to rid the Barbican area of most of its historic buildings, the directors of the association have, initially at great risk to their own affairs, maintained a significant portfolio of properties, all of which they have refurbished and kept in good repair for half a century; thanks, therefore, are due to them on a number of counts, not least of which is their commissioning of this work and the establishment of their 50th Anniversary initiative - the South West Image Bank.

Created in 2007 to house a collection of some two million negatives, from the Western Morning News and Evening Herald, the Image Bank occupies the ground floor premises of 32 Looe Street and is managed by Stacey Dyer. There, a team of volunteers are working on setting up an accessible, internet-friendly, digitised version of the collection and anyone reading this who feels that they may be able to help in any way - with identification or other information and/or scanning - please contact the Image Bank on Plymouth (01752) 665445.

Thanks are also due directly to the Western Morning News & Herald, Sutton Harbour Company, Plymouth City Museum, The Plymouth & West Devon Records Office and the Plymouth Local Studies Library for access to their photographic collections, with special acknowledgement to the late Dorothy Goodridge who compiled an excellent post-war pictorial record of the Barbican area which she subsequently donated to the Museum. A good number of the of archive images come from one or other of these sources, a significant number also come from the author's own collection and all of the contemporary images, notably the photographic record of listed buildings, were taken by the author. Others to whom I am indebted for photographs include Duncan Godefroy, Roy Westlake, Robin Hoskins, Gillian Kempster, Daryl Jago, DG Dine and Miss I Austin. While every care has been taken to try and identify individual copyright holders the publishers would be happy to hear from anyone who has information concerning the copyright of any uncredited images.

I would also like to thank Jill Cutts for allowing me full use of her

Plymouth Barbican Association Directors at their 50th Anniversary luncheon, Summer 2007. Standing: Vic French (2003), Edward Keast (Managing Agent), Tony Golding (1982), David Buckingham (2003), Chris Robinson (1985), Douglas Fletcher (2003). Seated: David King (1995), David Colwill (1988), Peter Stedman (1957), Duncan Godefroy (1986). Not present Bill Hodges (1995). Year of appointment in brackets.

grandfather's notebooks - the two volumes of AS Parker's 1918 Barbican Survey - copies of which are held in the PWDRO.

Thanks too to Mike Stone in the City Planning Department and Mike Daniells, Plymouth's Historic Environment Officer.

For checking and proofing thanks to Peter Stedman, Duncan Godefroy, Walton Gale, Doreen Mole, Rob Warren, Bill Bugler, Laurie & Patricia Greathead and their daughter - my wife and publisher - Clare Robinson.

On the print and production front, thanks to Bob Mills, Paul Opie and the great team at Latimer Trend.

Chris Robinson *September 2007*

Plymouth Barbican Association's Property Portfolio
FOREWORD

29 Looe Street
Grade II

32 Looe Street
Grade II

33 Looe Street
Grade II

6 The Barbican
Grade II

7 Stokes Lane
PC

22 New Street
Grade II

25 The Parade
PC

34 New Street
Grade II*

35 New Street
Grade II

36 New Street
Grade II

37 New Street
Grade II

38 New Street
Grade II

39 New Street
Grade II

40 New Street
Grade II

The Plymouth Barbican Association Limited directors in 1966:

CJ (Jim) Woodrow
Humphrey Woollcombe
EN (Ted) Masson Phillips
Crispin Gill
Stanely Edgcumbe
HT Walton Gale
Roger Serpell

John Eliott
A Southcombe Parker
GA Blakey
Lord Foot
Hilary Cornish
Ernest English
Ronald Lawry

Peter Stedman
The Earl of Mount Edgcumbe
Rt Hon Isaac Foot PC
Gerald Whitmarsh
CP Brown
G Russell Dunn
(MJ Treleaven served1969-91)

With the exception of Peter Stedman and Walton Gale all the above deceased prior to2007

Elizabethan Gardens rear of 34-40 New Street.=

7

INTRODUCTION

ITV's Hornblower being filmed in New Street.

The story of Plymouth's Historic Barbican is a truly remarkable one and, while there are doubtless parallels with other ancient parts of other ancient cities, I cannot help but feel that, as in so many other aspects of Britain's colourful past, Plymouth's story is just that extra bit special.

The Barbican currently encompasses the largest area of cobbled streeting to survive in England, the Plymouth Barbican Association was one of the first and largest conservation bodies of its kind in the country and the area today is one of the prime drivers in Plymouth's appeal to tourists. Sporting a wonderful collection of more than 100 listed buildings representing over 500 years of history on a street plan that even Drake would recognise.

All this despite, or perhaps because of, the fact that the city was, per-acre and per-head of population, the most heavily bombed city in the country during the Second World War, and its losses, in human and material terms, were second to none.

Sir Patrick Abercrombie's celebrated Plan for Plymouth - the post -war planning blueprint produced in 1943 - two years before the war had ended, was radical in its approach to rebuilding the city centre, but was seemingly respectful of what the authors called the 'Historic Precinct'.

Careful consideration of their proposals however reveal that they paid little more than lip-service to the ancient area and after drawing a relatively random wall around the old quarter their 'Plan' actually involved the demolition of all but a handful of significant buildings. To that end they were singing from the same songsheet that the Local Authorities had in their Council Chamber.

In the 1920s and 1930s the City Fathers had, in the name of 'slum clearance', removed a great many of the Tudor and Jacobean buildings from the old part of town, more, in fact, than the Lufftwaffe destroyed in more than fifty air raids.

After the war, and with a new agenda - to rehouse the bombed out civilian population of Plymouth - the Local Authority renewed their assault on the 'Historic Precinct' and, in a series of moves that were seemingly in line with the 1943 Plan, again set about the demolition of our ancient heritage, dubbing the offending properties 'hovels … unfit for human habitation'.

Happily however there were various pockets of Plymouth people who didn't like what they saw happening around them; the Old Plymouth Society, the Junior Chamber of Commerce and a number of young War veterans - men in their twenties and thirties who had witnessed the horrors of battle and who had already shouldered heavy responsibilities ahead of their years. Gradually what had been a number of lone voices came together and, under the initial umberella of the Old Plymouth Society, they formed the Plymouth Barbican Association. They then challenged the Local Authority, they took them on, they called their bluff and they saved a significant chunk of the Barbican and encouraged others to follow in their wake.

Had they not done so, there is little doubt that the Barbican today would be little more than a sprawling 1950s council estate with few facilities, maybe one or two pubs, a community centre and a handful of incongruous old buildings. But nothing like the vibrant tourist honeypot it is today, with its bar and cafe culture, its art and craft shops and Elizabethan Gardens.

Over the last decade or so the Barbican has seen more inward investment than any other part of the City since the rebuilding of the City Centre after the war, notwithstanding the developments around the University, the Hospital and Drake Circus. There can be little doubt that none of this would have happened had the area been bulldozed and modernised in the 1950s.

Happily the collective Council psyche has now largely come into line with the Conservationists and in a draft Document produced this year (*Barbican Conservation Area Appraisal and management plan*, a final version of which is due out in December 2007) it was heartening to read that many of the views expressed here are now shared by officials working on behalf on the Local Authority.

Foremost among them the recognition that: Notte Street is too busy and divides the Conservation area in two and that is not a good thing; that the Magistrates Court is in the wrong place and should, one day in the future, come down and the original line of St Andrew Street be restored; that the flats that were built over the bottom of High Street (now known as Buckwell Street),'do not contribute positively to the character or appearance of the Parade; that ideally Southside Street be made more traffic free and the granite sets (cobbles) be reinstated and presses for imaginative and sensitive redevelopment of Breton Side coach station.

There are plenty of other 'sensitive' proposals mooted for the likes of Exchange Street car park and Commerical Wharf, all set in a context that should not detract from historical essence of the area.

Just how well the Local Authority pay heed to this document remains to be seen. It's interesting to note that during the writing of this book, the Civic Centre was awarded Grade II listed status by English Heritage and we now have the embarrassing situation whereby the Council are trying to convince everyone that the forty-five-year-old building is not worthy of the listing and is unfit for purpose and should be pulled down. In the same way that they failed to appreciate what they had in the Barbican fifty years ago, they now fail to see that in the Civic Centre, the Council House and, although it's not part of the current discussion, Royal Parade, Plymouth has one of the finest collections of 1950s architecture in the world, and, despite the national and international recognition conferred by English Heritage, they want to pull it down and sell the site to a developer so they can have a new 'answer to everything' at Bretonside.

At what cost … to our heritage, our future?

In many ways the debate is similar to the one that kicked around fifty years ago, and one hopes that 'it's not working properly we want a new one' argument will be seen for the foolish notion that it is. However as Southcombe Parker stated at an Old Plymouth Society meeting in the early fifties, before the Civic Centre was built:

'We all, as children, liked building up towers with bricks or cards for the sheer pleasure of knocking them down again. It seems this instinct is magnified in many grown-ups and that they receive as much pleasure as the children in knocking down … I was unaware that the instinct could be so strong.'

Clearly no-one knows what the future holds, but we do all owe it to ourselves and future generations to try and learn from the past so that we don't repeat the mistakes of previous generations. Hindsight is a wonderful thing and 'if we knew then what we know now' the world would be a different place for sure, however the ultimate purpose of this book is not so much to lament what we have lost but to celebrate what we have saved and to attempt to ensure its well-being for the future.

Having worked on the Barbican now for thirty years, I feel I know the area quite well, but, in the course of writing this book, I have found that there is still plenty to learn and that, furthermore, in compiling the photographic collection of all the listed buildings in the area I found myself looking at many of the wonderful properties here with fresh eyes.

It is a joy to be on the Barbican and to operate a business out of one of the few Grade II* buildings in this richly endowed part of the world and I hope that everyone who reads this tome and who think they know Plymouth will also take the time to have a fresh look at the area. Meanwhile for those for whom the area is new or unknown I hope you enjoy the story and further that if anything similar is threatened in your own neck of the woods, that you too are ready to make your voice heard.

Chris Robinson
October 2007 Plymouth,

Bretonside & North Quay, 1895

"… it is no question of expediency or feeling whether we shall preserve the buildings of past times or not. We have no right whatever to touch them. They are not ours. They belong partly to those who built them, and partly to all the generations of mankind who are to follow us."

John Ruskin in the *'Seven Lamps of Architecture'* 1849

"Plymouth! Old Plymouth! Mother of full forty Plymouths, up and down the wide world, that wear her memory in their names, write it in baptismal records of all their children, and before the date of every outward letter! This is the Mother Plymouth sitting by the sea."

American visitor Elihu Burritt in his *"Walk from London to Land's End"* 1865

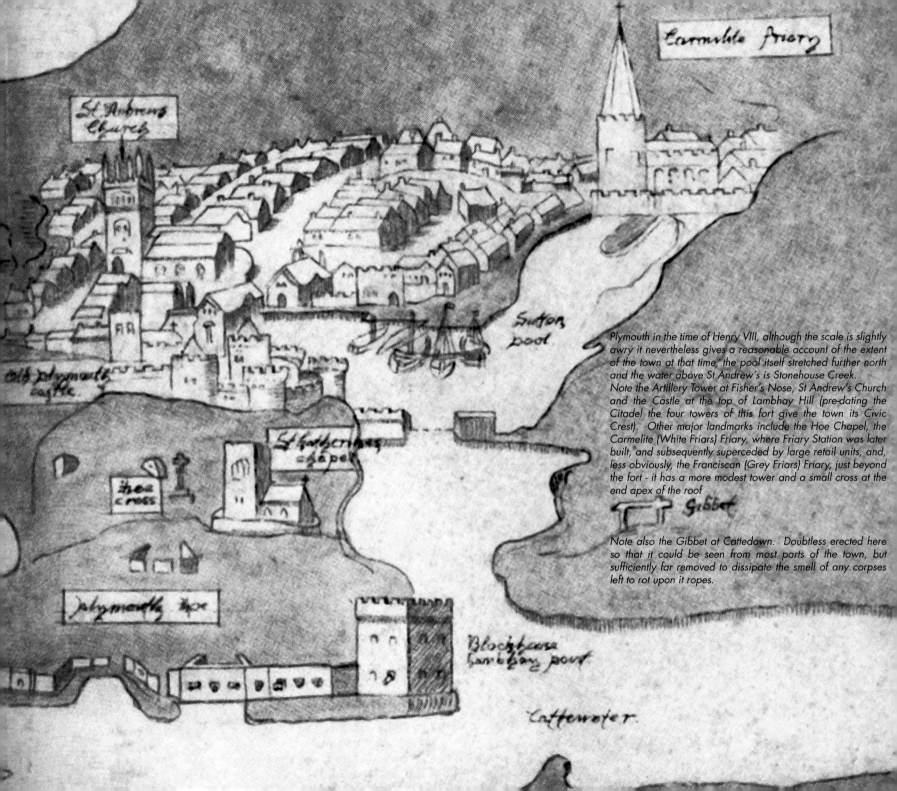

Carmelite Friary

St Andrews Church

Sutton Pool

Old Plymouth Castle

St Katherines chapel

Hoe cross

Plymouth in the time of Henry VIII, although the scale is slightly awry it nevertheless gives a reasonable account of the extent of the town at that time, the pool itself stretched further north and the water above St Andrew's is Stonehouse Creek.

Note the Artillery Tower at Fisher's Nose, St Andrew's Church and the Castle at the top of Lambhay Hill (pre-dating the Citadel the four towers of this fort give the town its Civic Crest). Other major landmarks include the Hoe Chapel, the Carmelite (White Friars) Friary, where Friary Station was later built, and subsequently superceded by large retail units, and, less obviously, the Franciscan (Grey Friars) Friary, just beyond the fort - it has a more modest tower and a small cross at the end apex of the roof

Gibbet

Note also the Gibbet at Cattedown. Doubtless erected here so that it could be seen from most parts of the town, but sufficiently far removed to dissipate the smell of any corpses left to rot upon it ropes.

Plymouth Hoe

Blockhouse Lambhay point

Cattewater

PLYMOUTH'S HISTORIC BARBICAN

Towards the end of March 1941 the Lufftwaffe, having waged intermittent aerial warfare on Plymouth over the previous nine months, dropped an enormous number of incendiary and high-explosive devices on the city over two frightening and unforgettable nights that are forever etched in the memories of those who lived through them. During the course of that terrible and terrifying bombardment some 20,000 properties were either destroyed or damaged, St Andrew's Church, Charles Church and many ecclesiastical edifices were reduced to shells, theatres and cinemas were lost, as were schools, libraries, halls and hospitals, and dozens of other public buildings. It was the first time in over 500 years that Plymouth had suffered directly at the hands of a foreign enemy, the last occasion having come at the dawn of the fifteenth century when Breton raiders had, according to the record books, spread fire through the town and burnt some 600 houses, a figure, which if it is to be believed, would have accounted for most of the town.

At that time, 1403, Plymouth, or Sutton, as it was still known, was a modest port of around 4,000 souls, nestled around the northern and western shores of Sutton Pool. Remarkably, the reconstructed town, occupied much the same footprint as it's pre-Breton counterpart and expanded but slowly until the period of great expansion under Queen Elizabeth in the second half of the sixteenth century.

It was Elizabeth's father, Henry VIII, who set the ball rolling with his Dissolution of the Monasteries. Plymouth had had two monasteries: one, an early fourteenth-century Cistercian 'Whitefriars' foundation on the north-eastern end of town, and the other, a late fourteenth-century Franciscan – Greyfriars – establishment to the south. In 1538 both were surrendered to the crown and by the 1580s both had passed into the hands of one of the leading entrepreneurial figures in Elizabethan Plymouth, John Sparke.

Previous pages: *The Barbican area in the early 1930s.*

The first Englishman to describe the potato – and tobacco – Sparke was Mayor of Plymouth twice, the first time just a year or so after Drake, in 1583. Sparke also appears to enjoy the distinction of being Plymouth's first property developer, or speculative builder, for New Street, it seems, was laid out as Mr Sparke's 'Newe Streete' with no specific purchaser in mind, just the knowledge that thanks to new money pouring into the town as a consequence of privateering (and pirateering) on the high seas, some wealthy sea captain would want a handsome house in this new part of town.

Essentially, most of the area below Notte Street and the bottom of High Street, on the south side of town – hence Southside Street – was laid out in the latter part of the sixteenth century and, remarkably, the principal areas of development from that glorious period in Plymouth's past managed to escape the worst excesses of the German bombing, leaving many architectural gems untouched. Untouched, but not untarnished. The reason that so many of these Elizabethan properties were still standing well into the twentieth century is that this had long since ceased to be a fashionable part of town. Other, older, areas - most notably around Old Town Street - had long since been redeveloped: this was where the new commercial heart of the nineteenth-century town had relocated, although here and there isolated properties survived well beyond their sell-by date.

To condense four hundred years of history into one paragraph however, what had happened back in the Elizabeth quarter, was that after almost two hundred years of yet more modest expansion after the death of Good Queen Bess, Plymouth, along with many other English towns and cities around the time of the Industrial Revolution, started to expand again. Money once again started to pour into the area and, with improved roads and transport, those that could afford to move outside the now congested

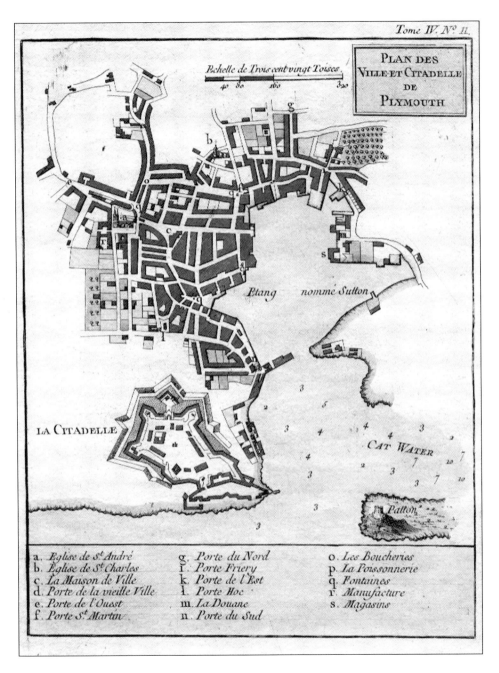

Tome IV. Nᵒ 11.

PLAN DES
VILLE ET CITADELLE
DE
PLYMOUTH

Echelle de Trois cent vingt Toises.

Etang   nomme Sutton

LA CITADELLE

CAT WATER

Patton.

a. *Eglise de St André*	g. *Porte du Nord*	o. *Les Boucheries*
b. *Eglise de St Charles*	i. *Porte Friery*	p. *La Poissonnerie*
c. *La Maison de Ville*	k. *Porte de l'Est*	q. *Fontaines*
d. *Porte de la vieille Ville*	l. *Porte Hoc*	r. *Manufacture*
e. *Porte de l'Ouest*	m. *La Douane*	s. *Magasins*
f. *Porte St Martin*	n. *Porte du Sud*	

confines of Sutton Harbour did just that, leaving the old, once-grand houses around the harbour shoreline to become multi-tenanted homes for much poorer people. And as the population doubled, tripled and eventually sextupled over the course of the nineteenth century so these houses got more and more crowded - with whole families living on just one floor, or, in worst cases, just one room of these no-longer spacious dwellings.

Unsanitary, infested and overcrowded, few landlords were interested in doing anything other than collecting the rent from these miserable hovels. Cholera found a ready breeding-ground here and by the time the nineteenth century was half way through John Sparke's New Street had 600 people living in its 43 houses, 26 of which had no privies or WCs. Plymouth, we are told, still had 30 cesspools around this time.

There had been a violent visitation of cholera across the area in 1832 with some 2,500 cases and over 1,000 deaths, 702 of them in Plymouth, including the Reverend James Carne, vicar of Charles Church and his wife. In 1849 there was another epidemic; '*It was first discovered on an emigrant ship, and spread rapidly through the overcrowded and insanitary parts of the Three Towns*' wrote FE Sach in his *Plymouth Book of Reference* in 1916. He also quoted the Rev George Prynne who was there at the time:

'*For three months we seemed to be living amongst the dying and the dead. A large wooden hospital for the whole of Plymouth was erected in our parish. We set up an altar in the largest ward, in order that everything might always be ready for communicating the dying. As the visitation reached its climax the deaths became very frequent and rapid. I was walking out one morning about nine o'clock. I met a woman hurrying along, and in answer to my enquiry she said she was going to fetch the doctor for her husband who had been seized with cholera. In the evening both she and her husband were in their coffins; the woman had died first!*'

Castle Street – or 'the Rag' - '*in which every house was formerly an inn and every inn a brothel*' – was typically pitiful and vulnerable despite its character having been '*mitigated as the result of the courageous interposition of the Rev Francis Barnes, who more than once entered its Infernos when nude men and women were dancing – causing the furies to decamp before his stern rebuke, and some landlords to disappear without removing their furniture,*' wrote Whitfeld in 1899. '*The former taverns were now tenanted by scores of families, and some houses accommodated sixty souls.*'

Left: Eighteenth-century, French map of Plymouth

Another of the old town's older streets was Lower Street. Here there were over 500 people living in fewer than 30 houses and there was one in particular, a once-grand property that boasted 24 rooms across three storeys that had 20 families living in it, a number that included 52 adults and 46 children … that's almost 100 people under one – doubtless draughty and leaking – roof. Nor were the rooms that big, most having been partitioned down to 5m x 4m or even smaller around 3m x 3m, and almost all of them doubling up as kitchen and bedrooms.

The situation was similar in Looe Street with the visiting Inspector from the General Board of Health, Robert Rawlinson reporting in 1853: *'The ground rises abruptly, and slippery half-worn limestone steps lead to houses more ruinous and more crowded than those fronting the street'.*

'Originally,' added Rawlinson, *'many of the houses now in ruins were erected as residences for the nobility and gentry of the town; but from being the abodes of those possessing wealth they now give partial shelter to the improvident, the vagrant, the vicious, and the unfortunate. The quaint carving on the stonework looks out of place; the walls are half in ruins; the gables are shattered, and foul weather stains of damp blotch the surface. Within, matters are even worse; the rooms are now divided and subdivided on every floor; the staircase is darkened; its massive handrail and carved balusters are crippled and broken; the once firm stairs are now rickety and dangerous; the stucco-finished plastering is blackened and in holes.'*

It was clear that something had to be done, and although remedial action was slow it tended to follow a consistent course of action; *'It is not long since, that in Higher Street, on the north side of Exeter Street, and Lower Street on the south side of the same street there could be seen numerous picturesque houses such as those shown in the accompanying sketch,'* wrote City Librarian, WHK Wright, in *The Streets of Old Plymouth* published in 1901.

He added: *'In common with nearly all the old streets of Plymouth the hand of the destroyer has been busy, and these fine gabled houses have been demolished to give place to newer and less picturesque dwellings. In this way old Plymouth is vanishing and new Plymouth is arising in all the glory of new bricks and ugly stucco to the disgust of lovers of the picturesque on the one hand, but to the joy of the utilitarian on the other.'*

It is sad that so many of these buildings managed to survive three hundred years with little or no investment (certainly towards the end of their days)

"It is not long since, that in Higher Street, on the north side of Exeter Street, and Lower Street on the south side of the same street there could be seen numerous picturesque houses such as those shown in the accompanying sketch." The sketch was of these buildings.

but fell almost wantonly at the end. Wright and his fellow 'lovers of the picturesque' were by no means the only ones lamenting their passing.

Reviewing the town's threatened heritage in his 1861 book *The Ancient Buildings of Plymouth* (a slender tome, the transcript of a talk delivered to the Plymouth Athenaeum in December 1860 which pre-dates any of the published histories of Plymouth), local architect James Hine was moved to pen this fanciful piece about *'that noble house in Notte Street'*;

The old house in Notte Street. Refashioned in the early 1880s.

"I fancy I see it in the course of erection; the masons and carpenters proceeding cautiously but skilfully with their work; the designer with watchful eye, testing the lines and details, and comparing them with the plan, which he measures with his great compasses. The burly alderman, in doublet and hose and ruffs, as he goes to and fro, gives an approving and patronising glance; and opposite a crowd of small fry is always stationed, looking on vacantly or wondering how much higher it is going. And when finished how well it looks, with its honest oak doors and windows, its diamond lights and high pitched roof, and inside its bold staircase, its panelled ceiling, and wainscoted walls. It was one of the best houses in the town. And was no doubt fitted with tapestries and Eastern carpets, massive tables, and high backed chairs and settles, cushioned with Utrecht velvet. Here and there a legend might have been written on the glass or walls. The whole interior was sombre yet cheery."

"Who knows? Perhaps Sir Walter Raleigh may have been entertained in this house, and (though less likely) Sir Francis Drake would have talked politics here. At Christmastide, its walls would ring with merry laughter, and madrigals and glees be sung around an open hearth."

Hine's picture, while purely a piece of supposition, nevertheless gives some idea of the setting into which this house was built and, it should be noted, Hine was writing in an attempt, not just to capture the imagination of the lover of the picturesque, but also to enlist the support of those who could see the value of such buildings to Plymouth as a whole. He is a prime candidate for Plymouth's first outspoken conservationist and his self-financed book was an attempt to alert the local population to a number of architectural and historical treasures that were under threat or altogether doomed.

It was almost certainly his hand that was behind a newspaper article that was published in July 1861 regarding what was then believed to have been the oldest house in Plymouth – the Turk's Head;

"I was designed and put upon my foundations rather more than 400 years ago, and have to thank the Crusaders, who beat the Infidels in the Holy War, for my name. In my youthful days the good town I'm about to quit for ever hadn't as many hundreds as it now has thousands of people, but it had more friars of orders grey, white and black, than there are parsons of every shade in all modern Plymouth. Some of them were early patrons of mine, and ever and anon gave me a call, liking well my sign, but better still my sack and my jovial company. A church, a monastery, and a town cross were my near neighbours, and I thrived well in their company; and of my surrounding contemporaries (solid, gabled, and mullioned, and put together much as I am), there was hardly one that kept its head (or tiles) much higher than mine, for the tall and overhanging timbered houses, like my old friend in Notte Street, had not yet been thought of."

Hine's protestations with regard to these key Plymouth buildings were to no avail, the house in Notte Street was, however, replaced by something seemingly sympathetic, albeit somewhat contrived.

The Turk's Head; St Andrew Street. demolished at the beginning of the 1860s.

A selection of the buildings that were cleared in the late 1860s to allow the construction of Plymouth's new Guildhall. Left: Looking up Catherine Street. Top: the Hospital of the Poor's Portion, Catherine Street (viewed from the south side of St Andrew's Church). Below that: the view of St Andrew's tower from the courtyard of the building. Other page, left: Basket Street and right: cottages at the top of Catherine Street.

Ruskin, the artist and art critic, whose *Seven Lamps of Architecture*, published in 1849, had been a seminal and most influential work on the issue of repair and restoration, would not have been impressed. For him restoration was *'the most total destruction which a building can suffer: a destruction out of which no remnants can be gathered: a destruction accompanied with false destruction of the thing destroyed.'*

Meanwhile, the Turk's Head was demolished and succeeded, on the same site, by a modern (Victorian) pub, the Abbey, its name being an allusion to another old property that Hine had singled out – the so-called Prysten House. Happily that building – the oldest domestic structure in old Plymouth – is still with us, probably on account of its enjoying a variety of commercial uses from the seventeenth to the twentieth century and therefore not falling foul of the typical rack-renting negligent landlords who ruined so many other notable old Plymouth buildings around the Barbican area in the late nineteenth century. Buildings like the early seventeenth-century Hospital of the Poor's Portion, which became the Workhouse, and which was demolished to make way for the new Guildhall in the late 1850s; the Hospital of Orphan's Aid, erected in 1615 and converted to the Grammar School forty years later and also sacrificed to make way for the new Guildhall at the top of Catherine Street. The same development also consigned the whole of the ancient thoroughfare known once as Love Street (it was a lover's lane on the western edge of town) or Basket Street as it was more recently known to the demolition men (the rebuilt Basket Street bore little resemblance).

The Hoe Gate; taken down in 1863.

Earlier in the 1860s another landmark structure, *'the Hoe Gate, the last of its race'* was also lost. Built in the sixteenth century and rebuilt in the seventeenth, it was leased by the Corporation in 1657 *'but ultimately passed into the hands of Mr TW Fox, who caused its destruction in 1863 – despite strong expressions of public opinion,'* wrote WHK Wright in his 1878 *Handbook to Plymouth, Stonehouse and Devonport*, adding: *'for it does appear something like an act of vandalism to remove so ornamental a structure, especially as the street itself is not a much-used thoroughfare.'*

As 'Perambulator' noted some years before its removal, in 1833, in the December edition of a short-lived publication called the *South Devon Monthly Museum*:

'With our love for specimens of ancient architecture commemorative as they are of events in our former history, yet we would not carry this veneration so far as not to give way to the increased demands of our modern society for further accommodation in our streets, and avenues to our town; to satisfy an increased population, using carriages of all descriptions in a way our ancestors neither did nor could use.'

This, of course, was long before the advent of the motor car, the double-decker bus and the articulated lorry: - one wonders what Perambulator would have made of Hoe Gate Street today?

Of course nothing stays the same forever and these were by no means the first venerable Plymouth buildings to have been pulled down in the nineteenth century in the name of progress: the old Mitre or Abbey in Winchelsea Street (later Woolster Street, later still Vauxhall Street) was pulled down to make way for the Exchange in 1812. John Harris, who in 1806 began writing an *Essay Toward the History of Plymouth* (yet to be made commercially available but quite possibly the earliest attempt to write a history of the town), described the building in great detail, and, one suspects, was very sad to see this, maybe, medieval building go. The notion of conservation, however, was neither widespread nor well-articulated at that time, and even Hine, fifty years on, found few supporters.

In the late 1870s the surviving remnants of the Whitefriars establishment were swept away to welcome the new Friary Railway Station and in 1880, despite a lively campaign waged by a number of eminent local figures, *'the most picturesque house in the town'* was pulled down - Palace Court. It seems remarkable now that this noble property should have been swept aside so easily. After all it would appear that this was the very house that the sixteen-year-old Catherine of Aragon was entertained in, for two weeks, on arriving in England in October 1501, prior to setting out for London and marriage to Henry VII's eldest son, Arthur – and which almost 400 years later still boasted many of its original features, However this was no longer the grand residence belonging to 'Master Paynter', five times mayor of Plymouth, rather it had become one of the worst slums in the town, its proprietors having *'fitted it up with as many miserable rooms for as many miserable people as can be crowded into it.'*

As another former Plymouth Librarian and author of the *History of Plymouth*, Llewelyn Jewitt, wrote in 1873:

'Palace Court, entered by an arched doorway, is situated in Catte-street, not far from the Old Guildhall, and is, at the present time, so far removed from anything palatial in appearance, or, in fact, that it has simply become the residence – being let off in separate floors and rooms – of people of the very lowest ranks of society. It is, indeed, a place to be but once visited, and that, a visit of but short duration. Still, putting aside all feelings of disgust at the modes of living of its denizens, or of the filth and squalor of the place, it is worth a visit, and some few interesting features will repay examination – especially a carved corbel on the landing of one of the principal staircases.'

WHK Wright agreed, in his Handbook in 1878 he recorded grimly that: *'... even as we write the fiat has gone forth ordering its demolition. A few weeks will probably see that insatiable monster "the School Board" in possession of the site, and calmly preparing for the erection thereon, of a modern board school, on ground which has been sacred to the memory of Royalty for nearly four centuries. Such is the order of things, however; the old must vanish and the new take its place, only to be superseded in its turn, after the lapse of years.'*

This was the cycle that the newly formed – in March 1877 – Society for the Protection of Ancient Buildings, were determined to break. Working with, and heavily influenced by, John Ruskin, William Morris wrote in the Society's Manifesto:

'If it be asked us to specify what kind of amount of art, style or other interest in a building makes it worth protecting, we answer, anything which can be looked on as artistic, picturesque, historical, antique or substantial:

Palace Court where Catherine of Aragon is reputed to have stayed when she first arrived in England from Spain. It was pulled down in the 1870s.

any work, in short, over which educated, artistic people would think it worthwhile to argue at all.'

To that end the fledgling society, somewhat ahead of their time, were keen to stress the importance of Protection ahead of Restoration, so obvious to us today, in much the same way as the medical profession now promote Prevention ahead of Remedy and Surgery. Morris's words are every bit as pertinent now as they were then, as he encouraged all who would listen to: *'...stave off decay by daily care, to prop a perilous wall or mend a leaky roof by such means as are obviously meant for support or covering, and show no pretence of other art, and otherwise resist all tampering with either the fabric or ornament of the building as it stands.'*

As it transpired, Wright was right, Palace Court was demolished. There were one or two of a professed artistic disposition that weren't entirely sorry: *'Although we are fain to regret the necessity which compelled the removal of this fine old relic of ancient Plymouth,'* wrote John McDonald in his *Nooks and Corners of Old Plymouth*, immediately after quoting Hine's wistful observations at length, *'we must submit that the building which at present occupies the site is more useful, more healthful, and in some respects more presentable than its predecessor.'*

Sadly for the newly-built Palace Court Board School a lifespan of three-score years and ten was all it could look forward to. Badly damaged by aerial bombing in the Second World War, it was subsequently reconstructed as an annex of the School of Art. All in all it had been a sad end for the fine old property, a building which was, *'even to the end, a place of considerable pretensions to dignity:*

Entering through an arched doorway at the High Street end of Stillman Street, the visitor found himself in a spacious quadrangle, with quaint buildings on every side. Arched doorways gave entrance to the various portions of the building, and even, when most dilapidated, there were to be found in the staircases, the windows, and the rooms, fine old carvings and charming wood panellings. Despite the squalor of the surroundings and the general air of dirt and dilapidation, the old building retained, to the last, signs of its former grandeur, both externally and internally.'

DISAPPEARING AXE

Cookworthy's house in Notte Street, demolished in the 1880s

Fond tributes from local antiquarians notwithstanding, and unable to bring Palace Court back from the rubble, our architect friend, James Hine was anxious to focus local attention on another endangered piece of town's historic past:

"The finest house in Plymouth of the Queen Anne period is one in Notte Street … set back from the street. The front is entirely of Portland stone, and details are exceedingly good. Here lived for many years (and died) Cookworthy, of china-clay and Plymouth pottery fame. Can you picture him, the quiet Quaker in his drab suit, seated in his wainscoted parlour before the fire-place with its blue and white Dutch tiles? The house is unique in its way, and nothing half so good will replace it."

Hine's open letter to the local press appeared in November 1882; what he didn't say, however, was that this grand edifice, referred to in the deeds as 'Old Mayoralty House' had also become multi-tenanted and very dilapidated. In recent years its fine doorway had been blocked up and the windows on either side of the door had been opened up as separate entrances, each approached by a flight of eight steps; however, the reason for Hine's impassioned outburst was that he knew that the old Cookworthy house was about to be demolished.

Earlier in the year, March 1882, Isaac Foot senior, had bought the building with the intention of demolishing it and constructing a Christian Mission Hall in front of it, which is exactly what he did, although he did preserve the impressive sculpted lintels and he retained part of the original front wall (which now found itself at the very back of the 'new' property). It was a sad end to a building that had had such a distinguished owner - and guests – Cookworthy entertained Captain Cook, James Smeaton and many other leading lights of his day here. The house had also served the town at other times as the Mayoralty House. Sadly, however, significant historical associations are seldom sufficient to stay the executioner's hand and money is generally at the root of all axe wielding.

Indeed, only the previous year, 1881, had seen a number of ancient properties on the north side of Stillman Street removed in order to build a new malthouse for Messrs Pitts and Co. Among them the house that the great biblical scholar, John Kitto, had been born in at the beginning of the nineteenth century. Kitto was, however, by no means a typical nineteenth century scholar, and his birth here does not suggest that Stillman Street was enjoying better fortunes than its immediate neighbours. Helping his father working on repairs to a house in Batter Street, young John slipped and fell 35 feet from a ladder and, after two weeks of being unconscious, awoke

This page, bottom: *the Salutation Inn, in Stillman Street*. Right: *John Kitto's house in Stillman Street - demolished c.1880*.
Opposite page: *Lambhay Street and the alleged castle remains*.

to find he had lost his hearing. This drove Kitto further into the world of books and although his parents could not cope with or keep him – he was forced to spend some time in the workhouse – his reading led to friendships that ultimately steered him to success as a writer: *The Pictorial Bible* and *The Encyclopedia of Biblical Literature*, were among his successes.

Despite his comparatively recent rise to national recognition (it was a German university that conferred a doctorate on him), Kitto's old house was pulled down less than thirty years after his death. By way of acknowledging his importance however we learn from Wright (*Streets of Old Plymouth*) that the 'proprietors of the site have affixed to their malt-house or store, a tablet bearing an inscription to the effect that Kitto was born in a house which formerly stood there.' The placement of this plaque was, according to Wright at that time (1901), *'the only instance we know of this being done in the town.'*

Curiously enough, however, in clearing this part of Stillman Street (first mentioned by name in 1412), a very ancient grave was found. An interment which was thought, 'in all probability', to have been the 'grave of one who lived in Devon after the Romans had visited our country, and introduced their mode of burial.'

Perhaps it was partly on the strength of this find that the British Archaeological Association visited the town in the summer of 1882. RN Worth, who chronicled the find and whose earlier *History of Plymouth* had been rush-released in 1872 to pre-empt Jewitt's – chaperoned a party of Association members around the old part of town, taking care to visit one of the other great Barbican buildings that is still with us, thanks largely to continuous commercial usage over the last two hundred years or so – the Distillery, in Southside Street.

Although Worth's suggestion that this was ever a house of Dominican or Black Friars is very much doubted, indeed the Domincans are not now thought to have been represented anywhere in the town, there can be no denying the antiquity of certain parts of the large and impressive distillery complex which has been the source of all Plymouth Gin since at least

1793. A candidate for the town's first Guildhall *'these premises may confidently be described as the oldest existing in the town,'* wrote Wright in 1899. Could its evident ecclesiastical features have come from the neighbouring Grey Friars establishment? Certainly it was usual to recycle stonework - particularly window mullions and doorways - when old buildings were pulled down and as there is little or no trace of the old monastery in New Street itself, perhaps when that site was cleared for John Sparke to lay out his said 'newe streete' at the end of the sixteenth century, some of that masonry found its way here. Whatever its provenance, the building's survival into modern times has rested, almost entirely, on the building's success as a distillery.

In much the same way the Citadel has survived in excellent condition and with little overall alteration on account of its being in continuous military occupation for almost 350 years. Indeed it almost seems too obvious to mention, but the Citadel is not only one of Plymouth's finest historic structures it is also one of the finest seventeenth-century fortifications in Europe. However, it was by no means the first fortification put up to defend the town; there was an earlier castle constructed in Drake's time, part of which makes up the south-eastern corner of the Citadel, and even before that there was a medieval 'Castel quadrate' that stood *'on a rokky Hille* (Lambhay Hill) ... *having at each corner a great Round Tower.'*

Like the disappearing Grey Friars monastery, little or nothing still stands today. The stonework would not have been wasted though, and some may have gone into the Drake fort, yet more may have been plundered for the Citadel itself, while during the

eighteenth century it would seem that what was left of the stonework was pilfered and used in the construction of the small dwellings built around its remains as the numerous little courts that were built around Lambhay Hill all bore witness: Horn's Court, as well as Cooksley's, Camber's and Martin's all contained adapted fragments of some medieval structure. So too does the oldest surviving building in Lambhay Street – the mid-eighteenth century Fisherman's Arms – and the odd, rounded fragment at the bottom of Lambhay Street. Believed by some but not all (Plymouth's Archaeologist Keith Ray thought it was nineteenth-century) to have been part of the old castle's gatehouse, this strange structure served as a dwelling-house in the 1890s.

The old castle and its four towers, were, of course, the inspiration for the town's civic crest and as such it also, presumably soon after its initial demise, gave rise to the name of one Plymouth's older hostelries – the Old Four Castles.

Of its early history we know very little save that Thomas Pike was landlord in 1657, the year Oliver Cromwell was offered the English crown by Parliament under the terms of the 'Humble Petition and Advice'. Fearing the republicanism of the Army, Cromwell declined and in Plymouth three pounds and ten shillings was spent at the 'proclaymenge of his highness the Lord Protector of the Commonwealth of England'. Thomas Pike, at the Four Castles, struck a special token and ten trees were planted in the new Charles Church churchyard.

A busy coaching inn throughout the eighteenth century, the Old Four Castles was one of at least a dozen watering holes in the Old Town Street in the middle of the nineteenth century and therefore not only had the disadvantage of plenty of competition, it also was located in a street, outside the core Barbican area, where pressure for commercial space was running high. Consequently, along with the 'Old Town Inn' three doors up the road, the Old Four Castles was closed in 1895 and pulled down the following year. Interestingly enough, as Plymouth was spreading out around the middle of the nineteenth century, two of the town's newer streets had hostelries that reflected the modernisation mentality; there was the 'New Four Castles' in Russell Street, and the 'New Town Inn' in York Street, two Victorian thoroughfares both now buried beneath the modern city centre.

Meanwhile, back in the 1890s and back in the really old part of Plymouth, where overcrowding, and not commerce, was the driving concern, the problem in 'those reeking tenements' was that as 'some of the older haunts were swept away, overcrowding had intensified in others to which the evicted resorted.'

'Dust, rust and dry rot had claimed Looe Street for its own,

The Old Four Castles in Old Town Street, demolished in 1896.

and its dilapidated mansions yielded from £60 - £70 a year in rack rents. In Higher, Lower and Middle Lanes were clusters of tottering retreats for the infamous, and How Street was none other than a scattered and monstrous rookery.'

'When the existence of these plague spots was revealed, meetings were convened by the Mayor, an Artisans' Dwellings Company was formed, and their blocks of model dwellings were supplemented by others raised by Sir Edward Bates and Mr John Pethick. The movement was further stimulated in 1890, when Mr JT Bond, the Mayor, conducted a slumming tour which resulted in the condemnation of a large section of Looe Street. Provision was made for the displaced population at Prince Rock and the reconstructed area was opened in the Mayoralty of Alderman Pethick in 1898.' (Whitfeld 1899)

How Street was completely transformed while Looe Street became, quite literally, a street of two halves.

'Looe Street is now almost a thing of the past; one side has been entirely demolished, and many of the old houses which in former days made the narrow thoroughfare so picturesque have been modernized and there is little or nothing now to attract visitors, save and except two or three quaint relics of Tudor architecture.' (Wright 1901)

Thankfully, the building-height line was more or less maintained, but clearly the street line was widened and a number of shops and pubs were lost and the character of the street compromised accordingly as the old timber-framed structures gave way to the modern council dwellings.

It would appear that little or no part of these old overcrowded houses was saved. In his book, *Sutton Harbour*, Crispin Gill recounts the story of how the local authorities decided to celebrate Queen Victoria's Diamond Jubilee (1897) with, amongst other things, an enormous bonfire on the Hoe – a bonfire built with timber from the condemned houses of Looe Street and How Street.

The buildings on the right here were pulled down in the 1890s. Corporation Flats were then built on this side of the widened thoroughfare.

"The Mayor and Aldermen and Councillors with their families all had the front seats; when the flames bit into the ancient timbers all their insect population flew for shelter, to the complete discomfort of the civic dignitaries."

The fleas weren't the only ones to flee the scene!

Incidentally, fire was another hazard that helped seal the fate of that part of Looe Street. It was two weeks before Christmas, 1885, in the early hours of Sunday 12 December, and: *'... the many inmates of No.3 Looe Street had just retired to rest when the alarm rang out, and flames belched from every window. There were from sixty to seventy people living in the house; and as the neighbourhood was thickly populated, consternation was general. The majority of inmates escaped by jumping from the window nearest to the pavement. Others who were aroused too late hung from the sills until the heat caused them to relax their grip, and they dropped with dull thuds to the pavement. An infant was thrown out by its father to the crowd and caught without injury. In all twelve lives were lost, one woman and her seven children being suffocated in a single apartment'* (Whitfeld: *Plymouth and Devonport in times of War and Peace*)

Needless to say, there was no national Fire Brigade service in 1885 and what provision there was, was generally dependent on whether insurance had been paid to cover such an eventuality.

The loss of half of Looe Street and the whole of How Street mirrored other changes in the area, as Worth noted in 1890: *'... to the Commissioners Plymouth is indebted for the improvement of Treville Street at a cost of £15,000, and for the widening of Whimple Street, from fifteen feet in its narrowest part to thirty-five"* ... *"where the streets, old and narrow, proved utterly inadequate for the reception of the traffic to and from the quays, great attention has wisely been paid. Notte Street and Woolster Streets have been widened almost throughout their whole length. Southside Street and Vauxhall Streets have received little less care ...'*

Here then was the man bemoaning the fact that *"Plymouth does not possess many features of archaeological interest"* congratulating the authorities on its modernisation programme.

'Some thirty years since it was pointed out by a careful and competent observer (presumably James Hine) that the town was not rich in architectural antiquities,' he added. *'Since that date fully half of those which remained have disappeared, and live but in remembrance.'*

Worth was writing his revised history (the third edition), just before Christmas 1890, before How Street and half of Looe Street were swept away, and it's odd that despite his obvious interest in the past, he appears to have had little inclination to actively campaign for its preservation.

Wright, in 1901, talks of how St Andrew Street was also: *'... until recently, full of old-world interest. Within living memory it contained some good specimens of Tudor architecture, and some of the best examples in the town. With their high gabled roofs, and projecting upper stories, these old houses formed a picturesque feature in the street architecture of Plymouth. One side of this fine old street has been entirely removed, but on the other, or west side, are still to be found some notable examples of ancient buildings.'*

'A short time since an old building was removed to make room for a modern factory, and when the site was cleared there was disclosed an entirely unknown aspect of this fine old mansion, its quaint windows and massive chimney stacks revealing the fact that it was in old times a building of considerable importance.'

Nor was it just in Plymouth that such concerns were being raised. Five years earlier, in 1896, the Society for the Protection of Ancient Buildings had hosted a conference in London, in conjunction with the County Council there, to consider the ancient buildings of the metropolis:

Opposite page: *Looe Street prior to the demolition of the northern (left) side of the street in the 1890s.*
Right: *St Andrew Street in the 1890s.*

'Londoners are by no means well informed as to the architectural treasures they possess.'

A proposal that a register of ancient buildings would help raise awareness and lessen the losses was proposed and accepted. That same year the National Trust bought, for the princely sum of £10, their first historic house – the fourteenth-century Alfriston Clergy House in East Sussex. The Trust, mooted a decade earlier, had come together through the efforts of the social reformer and acquaintance of Ruskin, Octavia Hill; solicitor Robert Hunter, who was also the lawyer for the Commons' Preservation Society founded in 1865 (Octavia Hill was its treasurer); and Canon Harwicke Rawnsley, an environmentalist friend of Hill, Hunter and Beatrix Potter, with a keen interest in the Lake District. Formally formed at the beginning of 1895, the Trust were given their first land that same year, four-and-a-half acres of Welsh coastland. Curiously enough the Commons Preservation Society is now a part of the William Morris Society.

The main aim of Hill, Hunter and Rawnsley's new National Trust for Places of Historic Interest and Natural Beauty, was 'to set aside the best and most beautiful parts of Britain for the public and prosperity, and to provide sitting rooms for the poor in the countryside.' And while the focus of the Trust was undoubtedly rural, the ideals of this new organisation and the work of the Society for the Protection of Ancient Buildings in London, were not without their impact in urban areas, and doubtless the latter's decision to compile a register of ancient buildings had some influence on Eldred and Wright's decision to take stock of Plymouth's old properties, not just those still standing, but including those lost within living memory, as if to emphasise the danger that our existing treasures faced;

'Two characteristic forces of the times which go hand in hand are the destruction of the picturesque and the creation of the hideous. This sweeping assertion … is made under great provocation. The few traces of the past which stand upon the ground whereon old Plymouth stood are getting fewer day by day. As one by one the old gabled houses vanish, so the ghosts which haunt them are laid, and the legendary or historic associations of a spot become forgotten when a factory smoke-stack marks the site. These however are signs which denote a town's increasing prosperity.'

'Unhappily," he said, echoing one or two of his peers, *'the old streets where once the wealthy merchants of the town resided have degenerated into a region of courts and alleys and decaying tenements given over to squalor and poverty. From crazy casements peer unwholesome faces – too often of women – slovenly, bloated, and unkempt. The sky-line of the roof-ridge suggests a wave of the sea. The plaster is falling from the walls in flakes. The windows lean awry in every direction, and the whole tottering structure is only saved from falling like a pack of cards by a stout warehouse at its side, against which it leans incapable of self-support.'*

'A lamentable state of things, truly; but observe the remedy.'

'The old houses disappear, to be replaced by a red brick foundry or factory. From the confines of the town there shoot forth endless rows of hastily built dwellings in unsightly and monotonous sequence. They stretch and multiply like the limbs of some foul hydra, poisoning what they cannot devour of field and hedgerow.'

But it's one of life's little ironies, as we've travelled down the 'so-called' path of progress that that path, of necessity, has had to cover more and more green-field sites to accommodate the expanding population and those existing and old paths have to become wider and wider to accommodate each development in transport. At first on foot; 'shanks's pony', walking on one's own legs (shanks), is an expression that comes down to us from the eighteenth century, which was a time when the turnpike acts were making roads ever more suitable for wheeled vehicles – carts and carriages. It's worth noting that once the Romans had left the quality of road construction in this country was set back several centuries.

As the nineteenth century unfolded and such wheeled transportation, notably the introduction of the two-wheeled, horse-drawn Hansom cab in 1834, so the speed of movement around towns, up and down the country, increased, leading to further road surface improvements and thus the possibility of yet heavier vehicles, road rails initially paving the way for the development of the tram. These too were horse-drawn at first but it wasn't long before stretches had become powered by electricity, necessitating changes above ground as well as on it. A photograph in the archives of the local newspaper shows the junction of Ebrington Street and Old Town Street in the course of partial demolition and on the back someone has scribbled 'Plymouth during the blitz' the assumption clearly being that rubble equals bomb damage. The picture, however, was taken more than forty years earlier and chronicles the widening of the junction to accommodate the new electric tram route.

The internal combustion engine brought ever-increasing demands on our roads as two lanes, allowing traffic to move freely in both directions, were no longer sufficient, room was needed now for unloading and overtaking and so on ... All of which, when combined with the commercial pressures to provide as much accommodation as close as possible to the heart of community – 'location, location, location,' as the estate agents advise their commercial customers – meant that changes to the old world were inevitable:

'In Pins Lane formerly stood the quaint little houses shewn having outside staircases and old diamond-paned windows. They had become very dilapidated and were very insanitary, consequently their removal was necessary. Nevertheless, one cannot but regret that so picturesque a bit of old Plymouth could not have been preserved.'

The situation wasn't entirely hopeless, however, and here and there Eldred and Wright were able to throw welcome light on some of the old town's surviving dark corners:

'Few people, perhaps, who pass down High Street towards the quays realise that for centuries this old thoroughfare was the principal street of Plymouth. Long before George Street or Bedford Street were known (both of them incidentally destined to be casualties of the war just forty years after this was written), centuries before Union Street emerged from the marshes, the High Street of Plymouth was the very heart and centre of the famous old town. Up and down this street the brave men who helped to make the history of Elizabethan days passed and repassed, exchanging greetings with friends and comrades, and perchance, holding revel in one or other of the taverns or houses of call with which the neighbourhood abounded.'

'Little do the dwellers in the now squalid tenements and crowded courts imagine that generations of fair women and brave men lived and loved in what were in those olden days mansions, and are now the mere backwaters of the prosperous life of the modern progressive town. Here in what are now designated the slums, lived the merchant princes and the men of light and leading of their day and there were many prosperous traders who carried on their avocations in Plymouth's High Street.'

'It is even now picturesque, but squalor goes hand in hand with the signs

The cellar and solar buildings in Pin Lane, pulled down in the 1890s.

of ancient dignity, and decay is visible everywhere. Nevertheless it is still High Street, and to those who are interested in it for old time's sake, it is still reminiscent of those older Elizabethan days. For a time its name was changed, and it was known as Market Street, the market, or a portion of it, being carried on beneath the Old Guildhall which stood at the top; its successor, in fact, stands there still as a witness and landmark of past generations, although its character is altered.

'In dealing with such a subject as this, one feels that ordinary prosaic language is not sufficiently expressive; romance is in the very air, the whole neighbourhood teems with suggestions of ancient days; of the vanished glory and dignity of this old street, and of those who frequented it in the by-gone ages. We can picture ourselves Drake the intrepid, whose town house was not far away, the courtly and chivalrous Raleigh, who, on his visits to Plymouth, is supposed to have lodged in Notte Street, the bluff old sea-dog Hawkins who probably had a house in this very street; and all the other great sea captains of a wondrous age, swaggering up and down "wearing out the Pebles," as Davenant puts it' [A reference to a seventeenth-century play by Sir William Davenant, *Newes from Plymouth*, which makes mention of High Street]

'One of the relics of the past which will attract the antiquarian student who ventures to penetrate into one of the arched recesses on the right side of the street, going down towards the quays, is what is known as Nicholl's Court. Here will be found a series of stone arches which evidently indicate the entrance to some fine old mansion, whose, or even of what particular period there is no evidence to determine.'

New Street too, still had a Tudor air about it:

'Although called New Street it is one of the oldest streets in the town, and was, in the eighteenth century, the residential quarter of some of the principal merchants and people of standing in the town. It had, however, very much deteriorated in the early part of the nineteenth century and has gradually gone lower in the social scale of its inhabitants, as well as in the rickety character of its buildings. Two houses with fine overhanging gables and carved corbels and doorposts, are solitary specimens of what Plymouth houses used to be, and even they are doomed.'

Or at least so it appeared in 1901.

Opposite page: *High Street looking south.* This page, left: *New Street.* Above: *High Street looking north.*

Front cover of Sibyl Jerram's book of sketches, 1913.

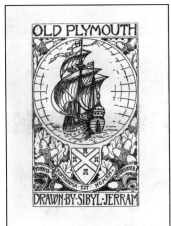

Southcombe Parker's 'Civic Survey'. Note the Archaeological Survey has been crossed through and changed to Anitquarian. Right; typical pages from the two books.

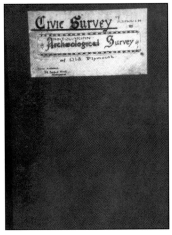

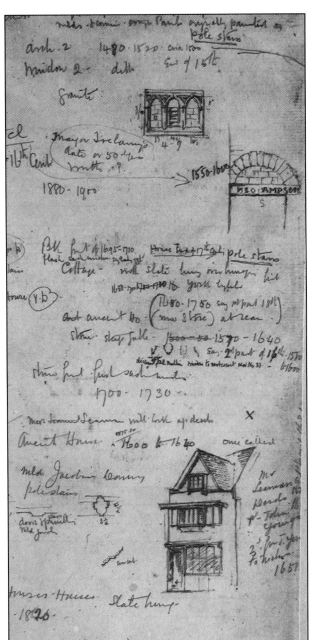

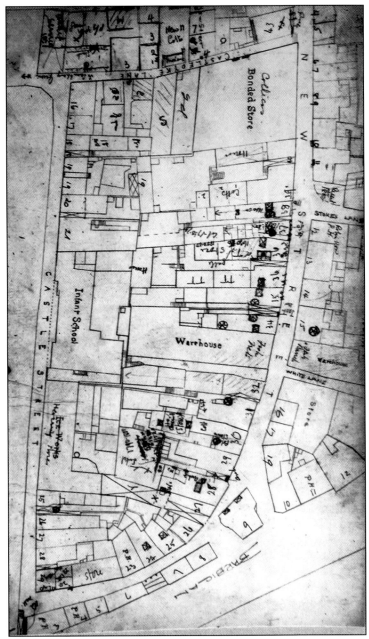

THE TIDE TURNS:
THE BATTLE FOR THE ELIZABETHAN HOUSE

The last quote there came from Sir Philip Pilditch, who further wrote that he had 'had the good fortune' to have a look at Southcombe Parker's unpublished sketchbooks and 'I saw at once that there was a great deal more in the city than I had thought which demanded consideration.'

Born in Exeter in 1865, Southcombe Parker had gone to Exeter School of Art and Science in 1879 and five years later passed the SK Honours Building Construction exam, coming first in the whole of England. Having simultaneously served his articles with James Crocker in Exeter, he thereafter spent the next few years working with architects in Eastbourne, Derby, Leicester, Newcastle and Marlborough, before coming to Plymouth in 1891 as the personal assistant to the architect HJ Snell. Southcombe Parker spent five years with Snell finding time within that period to instigate a movement in Exeter for the retention of ancient buildings and the marking of historic places and sites by tablets.

He also, in conjunction with his first employer, James Crocker, helped set up the Devon and Exeter Architectural Society, with a specific offshoot in Plymouth. And it was in Plymouth, in 1896, that Southcombe Parker set up his own practice. Over the next few decades he would design and see through the construction of many notable buildings in the area – among them the erstwhile George Street Baptist Church and Plymouth Institution Library, the Lloyds Bank block for the Duke of Bedford in Tavistock and a number of buildings in the High Street, Totnes. He also completed a number of commercial premises and domestic residences as well as maintaining his interest in old buildings.

A passionate advocate of the Plymouth Building By-Laws, the amended legislation, when passed in 1909, was largely his work. For many years building curator of the Plymouth Institution, he acted as Chairman of the Plymouth Civic Survey when the body, which was made up of architects and engineers too old for military service, completed, in 1918, 'particulars and plans for the improvement of the city'; suggestions which included the purchase of an area bordered by Alma Road, Tavistock Road (Outland Road) and Peverell Park Road, before any more building should take place. Approved by the Corporation this was the effective birth of Central Park.

Southcombe Parker's committee also commissioned a map and brought up to date a large relief model of the surrounding countryside that had been made by the War Office in 1885. However, it was his own idiosyncratic, hand-drawn, survey of the old parts of Plymouth, that was perhaps destined,

Even though they were clearly aware that their book, and the sentiments expressed within it, were by no means likely to reach a mass audience (there were only 350 copies printed), Eldred and Wright weren't the only ones locally interested in recording Plymouth's then little-known architectural treasures. Local artist John McDonald had produced an earlier, limited-market, publication featuring his own drawings of *The Nooks and Corners of Old Plymouth* in 1883 (the Earl of Mount Edgcumbe, several councillors and local historians: Brooking-Rowe, WHK Wright and RN Worth were among the 100 subscribers), while Sibyl Jerram, thirty years later, in 1913 compiled a similar, more detailed collection of bits and pieces including drawings of doorways, alley ways, stairwells, fireplaces and cupboards, as well as exterior views of old Plymouth properties. Whether they were all inspired by Ruskin's earlier pronouncements is unclear, however, one man, Arthur Southcombe Parker, almost certainly was.

Writing in 1930 shortly after he had successfully masterminded the restoration of No.32 New Street – the first building in Plymouth to have been saved by direct public action – Southcombe Parker made a reference to 'the great Ruskin' - he was clearly a fan. Parker was also a fine architect and capable artist, and over a period of 'some years' he compiled *'a list of old things in various parts of the city worthy of looking into for the purpose of preservation'*.

albeit indirectly, to be his most enduring legacy to Plymouth. Completed during the same time period, 1914-18, the work fills two small, case-bound sketch books and is titled *Civic Survey of Greater Plymouth – Antiquarian Survey.*

There can be little doubt that all the sketches were carried out on location and in addition to the obvious architectural front elevations of properties there are a wealth of architectural details – ceilings, staircases, covings, balustrading, door frames, window frames and corner cupboards – if anyone knew what sixteenth and seventeenth-century remnants there were in twentieth-century Plymouth it was Arthur Southcombe Parker. Furthermore, it is likely that there was no one more acutely aware of just how threatened that inheritance was.

Realising that there was little or no chance of all that he recorded being preserved for prosperity, ASP coded each of his observations with a three-tier assessment of their respective worth. The first category were simply worthy by dint of their being within the catchment area, the second were scored 'D' meaning 'desirable', and the third tier were marked 'VD' – 'very desirable'. By 'very desirable' he certainly wasn't using the term in modern estate agents parlance of this or that property being a 'des res' – desirable residence – for these houses, for the most part, were anything but desirable residences as he pencil-picked his way around them. Rather they were 'very desirable' from a conservation perspective. Imagine his horror, therefore, one day, six or seven years later, when he saw a notice placed in the Western Independent inviting tenders for the razing of one of his VD selections – No.32 New Street.

"There being no Society that could act – I took it upon myself to write to the Society for the Protection of Ancient Buildings, in London, for their help,' recalled Southcombe Parker in 1943. 'Mr AR Powys came to Plymouth, and again several times afterwards on general matters. A letter was written to the Corporation asking them to hold up the procedure – which they did. The tenders were high – I might say that several letters sent from London were written in Plymouth.'

'A temporary Society or Committee, known as the Old Plymouth Fund, was formed with Mr Richard Winnicott as Chairman and Mr JJ Judge as Hon Treasurer.'

Left: *The Elizabethan House in 1928, note the broken windows.*
Right: *Looking down New Street shortly after the restoration of No.32.*

'He then enlisted the help of Lady Astor,' recalled his son, also Arthur Southcombe Parker, some years later.

'Together they raised £100 and purchased the house, which was in such a perilous state that shortly after the purchase the roof fell in. Father gave his architectural services without charge. He used old roofing slates cut small to conform to those used in the 16th century. Especially by moonlight the slates had the appearance of fish scales.'

Securing the property and ensuring that it was watertight was, however, just the beginning. There was still a great deal of work to do and to enable that work to be done, a great deal of money had to be found. Hence the Old Plymouth Fund and the need to enlist the vocal and financial support of anyone in a position to help, especially people like Plymouth MP Lady Nancy Astor and the exiled Plymothian and Middlesex MP, Sir Philip Pilditch, who was contacted on this matter via the Plymouth Institution, who, it would appear, had copies of ASP's list of ancient houses.

Philip Pilditch was one of nine children born to a carpenter/builder from Thurlstone in 1861. Educated at the Reverend Dr Slater's North Hill Grammar School on North Hill, Plymouth, he completed his education at King's College, London and acquired something of a reputation for himself as an architect, surveyor and land agent, becoming consulting surveyor for the Duke of Bedford, Marquis of Bath, and others. After two unsuccessful attempts in 1906 and 1910, he was elected to the House of Commons in 1918 (for a Middlesex seat – he was also knighted that year for his public-service work and his efforts in funding local battalions in Surrey and Middlesex during the Great War) and became a specialist in finance, housing and town planning. In 1927 he played a large part in the shaping of the Landlord and Tenant Act. He also helped secure Hadrian's Wall for posterity, all of which placed him in an excellent position to support Southcombe Parker in his quest to save 32 New Street from demolition (Parker had also, incidentally, been instrumental in saving the old Custom House on the Parade from demolition the previous year – 1926).

'Destruction of the area,' wrote Pilditch in his profile-raising pamphlet of 1929 *Elizabethan Plymouth and Its Preservation 'seemed imminent'* ... but then *'the Society for the Protection of Ancient Buildings who, with Mr AS Parker, were the first to draw attention to the matter, proposed that one of these buildings, which has already been purchased by the Corporation, should, when restored, be devoted to the purpose of a Drake or Elizabethan Museum, and handed over to the care and charge of the Museum Committee of the Plymouth Corporation.'*

Two views of the lower part of New Street from this time.

Originally the plan had been to sweep away most of the perceived problem properties:

'Anyone walking through the place would have to admit that its condition has become in many respects deplorable. Not that the people are as unhealthy as these conditions would lead one to expect. Probably because the inhabitants live in the open air and only sleep in these poor tenements, the health of the people is not so bad, and there are,' he noted, 'many cases of longevity.'

'When,' he continued in the third person, 'the present writer went round the district with some of the authorities of the town, attention was drawn to the fact that in one small place there was not a single pane of glass left in the windows, and one of the officials supplied the information that there was a clean bill of health in that particular house. But Plymouth cannot let the present insanitary conditions go on as they are; they have probably been gradually getting worse since the writer, as a boy, used to wander about among them, dreaming of the Plymouth of the ancient days. And they were bad then.'

And yet: 'This little quarter is, in its way, as fine as anything in any town in England which retains any medieval association. If it were anywhere on the Riviera or Provence, or in Spain or Italy, English and American tourists would be found going into raptures over it, but here it is in drab old England, and we have not known how to make the most of it.'

Admittedly: 'anybody looking at the district now will certainly have to do so with an imaginative eye to see what it will look like when its present rather neglected appearance is changed by the cleansing, restoring, and colouring that will have to be done to bring out its latent charm, as some other towns (notably Hastings) have done to their old districts.'

But: '... nobody looking at those interesting little courts could say he would like to have a hand in their destruction, and face what the inhabitants would be likely to say to those who would remove them from their pleasant and individualistic surroundings, to rooms in great tenement buildings, the rents of which must be prohibitive to them, even when assisted by subsidies and the rates.'

As Pilditch explained, the clearance method as first proposed '...would have involved the demolition of the greater portion of all the houses, squares, courts, and cottages in the area bounded by Southside Street, the Barbican, Lambhay Street, Lambhay Green and Pins Lane, and including some of the most delightful old stone houses of mediaeval England, one or two dating from Drake's time, such as were illustrated in The Times of October 16th, and in the Western Morning News of October 29th, 1926.'

'That scheme would have involved obliteration of the lines of the old streets known as New Street and Castle Street and, among the courts, of Cambers and Cooksley courts which are on the slopes of the hill entered from Castle Street and Lambhay Street, and the building of great blocks of workmen's dwellings on the cleared area.'

'But, the course of events in the past few years has shown that Plymouth is capable of rising to the height of full realisation of what it possesses in this quarter, and what a valuable asset it is, not only to Plymouth, but to the whole of the English-speaking race.'

Stirring words from the man who opened his pamphlet with the news that: '... it has recently been made public that the scheme of reconditioning the

Elizabethan district of Plymouth, i.e. Old Plymouth, instead of razing the whole of it to the ground, as first proposed, having been adopted by the Corporation, has now been sanctioned, in principle, by the Ministry of Health, and, subject to the result of an inquiry recently held at Plymouth by a representative of that Ministry, will soon be an accomplished fact.'

Thus it was that Sir Philip was able to explain the 'scheme for retaining the lines of the streets in the whole area and the courtyards which give so much of its character to the district, repairing and reconditioning such of the houses as are proposed to be retained as dwellings, and removing from their rears the poor buildings which have grown up in more recent times, and obstruct a good deal of the light and air.'

'There will be several quite good sized open spaces, and in addition, it is proposed to erect a block of six flats of three rooms each on a site at the corner of Pin Lane; a block of three flats of two rooms each in Castle Street, and a block of twelve flats of two rooms each at the corner of Castle Street and New Street.'

'These blocks of flats are not intended to be excrescences but will work in as to frontage, and as much as possible, as to character with the rest of the buildings on the site.'

'This alternative "Sanitate but Save" proposal will undoubtedly necessitate the obtaining by the Corporation of sites not far away on which to house the portion of the population which would be dispossessed by it. But the same would occur to a very greater extent if new streets were cut through the area, destroying its character, and blocks of dwellings erected on the site.'

This then was the revised vision:

'A renovated Elizabethan district, its heart a museum in a house that Drake saw, the magnet to attract for all time mementoes concerning the greatest of Plymothians, and the old antique shops which should spring up in the vicinity, as they have elsewhere, would intensify the call that Plymouth Hoe and Sound have for the English, and bring visitors from all over England, and from the ends of the English-speaking world.'

It all seems so straightforward and logical from our present perspective, but, as if to emphasise just how hard won the battle had been, Sir Philip,

The Lord Mayor, Lieut-Col Drury, and Sir Philip Pilditch.

the consummate gentleman, concluded his piece with a metaphoric vote of thanks to those who stood behind the Elizabethan standard:

'Successive Mayors, Mr RJ Mitchell in 1926, his immediate predecessor Mr Alderman RW Winnicott, Mr Alderman JJH Moses in 1927, and Mr WHJ Priest in 1928, together with Alderman Lovell Dunstan, the Deputy Mayor, and Mr AE Webb, the very capable Chairman of the Housing Committee, have done their best to get over the serious difficulties, and the local press, i.e. the Western Morning News and the Western Independent, have given their most valuable support at all times. Plymouth is also much indebted to the indefatigable labours of Mr AR Powys, of the Society for the Preservation of Ancient Buildings, Mr AS Parker, and Mr JJ Judge, of Plymouth, as well as the Town Clerk, Surveyor, the Medical Officer, who has been very properly concerned for the health of the inhabitants, and others of the Borough, and of the Plymouth Institution. The Members of Parliament for Plymouth, Lady Astor, Sir A Shirley Benn, Bart., and Mr Hore Belisha, have shown practical sympathy with the idea.'

32, New St., Plymouth. Elizabethan period house which, when restored, is to be used as a Drake and Mayflower Museum.

Sir Philip's rallying call was designed to win yet more support. However as, when the pamphlet was published, work was not yet completed on the 'Museum' and, a little worryingly, more work had been done than had been paid for - or indeed than there was money available for – hence the original name of the committee formed to manage the whole affair: 'The Old Plymouth Fund'.

Sir Philip and Lady Pilditch (he was created a Baronet in 1929) generously pitched in 25 guineas and some ten other members of the Pilditch family between them added a further 12 guineas (around £1,500 in early twenty-first-century terms), one or two of the aforementioned Mayors were equally generous, Southcombe Parker, contributed 10 guineas, but most impressive of all was a gift of £200 (around £8,000) from Viscount and Viscountess Astor.

As of October 1929 that contribution from Plymouth's first couple represented more than a quarter of the donations made towards the estimated final total of around £1,200, and what made the gift all the more remarkable was the fact that it came hot on the heels of their very generous bequest that set up the Virginia House Settlement off Batter Street in December 1925 and the Astor Institute at Mount Gould in April 1929 (which was built at a cost of £10,000), not forgetting, a decade before that, the gift of the Astor Playing Fields off Embankment Road.

But it wasn't just financial support that the former Sutton MP and his wife, the sitting Sutton MP, offered the campaign, it was vocal support too. At the public meeting held on the Barbican Pier, on the afternoon of Friday 11 October 1929, to promote the Old Plymouth Fund, Viscountess Astor and Sir Philip Pilditch were the Chief Speakers. Mayor Ambrose Andrews was in the Chair and the stated object of the meeting was 'to interest Citizens in the progress of the Restoration of the Old House, 32 New Street'.

Although in a somewhat wretched state by 1927, 'practically the whole of the street front remained intact', according to Parker, who oversaw the work, and 'the whole of the structural framework, including walls, frame and roof timbers were all as originally built.'

'The principal adopted was retention of all Old Work supplemented with new where weak – but not destroying the Old. A large building in the garden was demolished, which added to the expense, and an Elizabethan Garden was planted in its place by Miss Mary Bayly.'

'The restoration itself was carried out by Ambrose Andrews – the Mayor of Plymouth,' added Parker, in his 1943 address, *'the street front is all original excepting the Door and the Ground Floor Mullions.'*

'There was difficulty about the door,' noted a report on a meeting of the Old Plymouth Fund executive, in the *Evening Herald* on 28 November 1929: *'Mr Parker had appealed to the committee of the Museum to allow them to have a door which was now in the Museum and which had been taken from a house in Looe-street. It so happened that that door fitted 32, New-street, but the Museum committee had refused them. Mr Parker said that that the door had probably stood in Looe-street for 200 or 300 years before it was placed in the Museum and he did not see why the door could not be well preserved and protected in New-street. It would still belong to the Museum, and would be more Elizabethan in actual position than placed against a wall.'* The committee did not agree.

Notwithstanding the Museum's attitude there was undoubtedly an air of moving forward with regard to the past however, and Southcombe Parker, together with Charles Bracken, was busy compiling a list of *'over 100 things still in Plymouth worth preserving'*.

It was at that November 1929 meeting that Bracken moved the resolution mooted by Sir Philip Pilditch that a new body should be formed – the Old Plymouth Society. Bracken was at that time the headmaster of Plymouth Corporation Grammar School, a post he had occupied for some twenty years. Back in 1927 he had published a *History of Plymouth Public School* and the following summer, 1930, in his sixty-second year, he would retire and accept a commission to produce a series of articles on the history of Plymouth. In the end he wrote fifty-six pieces and these, revised and extended in 1931, became the first edition of his *History of Plymouth and Her Neighbours*. A later historian of Plymouth, and founder member of the Barbican Association, Crispin Gill, was a pupil:

'I was among Charlie Bracken's pupils in 1930, in the third form. I remember him as a small dapper little man, very precise with his pince-nez but with a wonderful sense of humour. If a member of staff was away he would assemble several classes of like age into the hall and would talk to us for an hour or two on Plymouth history. Maybe it was here that my enthusiasm for the subject was born.'

Certainly Bracken and Parker - and Pilditch's - passion inspired a growing number of interested parties to get involved. Nevertheless they were still short of the amount needed to complete the work on No.32. It was Sir Philip's view that the last appeal, whereby 250 letters had been sent out and only 12 guineas had come in as a consequence, was not the way forward.

'There is only one way to get the money and that is by half-a-dozen people making a personal appeal to some of the big people in, or associated with, the city. We have to get hold of the people who have done or who are doing well out of Plymouth and make them realise what it means to restore these ancient buildings.'

He added: *'One is beginning now to realise that that out of the restoration of 32 New Street is growing into something much bigger than most of us anticipated, Plymouth is undoubtedly recognised all over the world. Its name awakened an echo all over the world, more than any other city, save, perhaps, Stratford-on-Avon.'*

'We have seriously neglected our heritage during the last fifty or a hundred years. We have allowed many glorious relics to be wantonly destroyed. Plymouth should be the great Elizabethan centre of England, but that fact has been somewhat lost sight of, and now we are hardly cognizant of what still exists in our midst. I have taken the trouble to prepare a list, and it is surprising to see what still remains.'

That list was almost certainly based on Southcombe Parker's *1914-18 Antiquarian Survey* and the Prysten House, 32 New Street and the Old Customs House were singled out, along with Mayflower (Island) House and houses in High Street, Notte Street, Woolster Street, Looe Street, Exeter Street, Kinterbury Street, Southside Street, Batter Street, Moon Street, Treville Street, Vauxhall Street and Norley Street. He then went on to mention various *'historical fragments'* which included the King Henry VIII towers, the Manor walls at Stonehouse, Budshead and, rather oddly in this section, the Old Ring of Bells pub. A reference to *'a third set of relics … such as mantelpieces, staircases, beautifully constructed chimneys and ceilings'* sounded distinctly Southcombe Parkeresque.

"These are priceless fragments," Sir Philip continued: *"and yet all they have in the museum are two doors, a ceiling, and a set of brackets. Hundreds of fragments must have disappeared during the last fifty years and will continue to do so unless something is done to save them. Unless something is done in this old city they will be lost, and the opportunity will be gone*

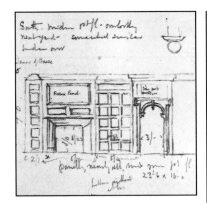

Sketches from Southcombe Parker's notebooks and (right) the Jacobean door. Top right; A room from the restored Elizabethan House.

RELIC OF TUDOR PLYMOUTH.

of making Plymouth the repository of the finest set of Elizabethan relics existing in the country. Is Plymouth going to tackle its old buildings, its old fragments, and those other items which should be in the museum?"

He urged that some body should be set up to take the work in hand. What was now needed was a complete survey of all the relics which remained. Have them listed and illustrated.

"We could," he said, knowing that this was part of the reason for convening the meeting, "form an Old Plymouth Society, with a branch in London." And that, of course, is precisely what happened.

On 17th January 1930, in front of a large audience in the Council Chamber, the Mayor, Alderman J Churchward, was appointed Patron of the Old Plymouth Society. Viscount Astor was made the Plymouth President, Sir Philip himself the London President, the Mayor was also to act as Chairman, Southcombe Parker and Charlie Bracken were to produce an inventory of Plymouth's architectural antiquities, Charles Cheverton, another architect, was given the title of Devonport correspondent, Lt-Col WP Drury, the Mayor of Saltash, was made Saltash correspondent and Southcombe Parker's son, and namesake, became the fledgling society's secretary. The treasurer was Captain Sydney Moon.

At the meeting Sir Philip spoke of the great importance of 'Mr AS Parker, FRIBA, to whom so much was due in connection with the maintenance both of the district and 32 New Street – the efforts made between 1925 and 1929," he said, "had resulted in the preservation of the old district as a whole and in the restoration of 32 New Street, a nucleus around which Elizabethan Plymouth would in future group itself … if it were not taken it is probable that most of what still remains would have disappeared in the course of a very few years.'

Sir Philip also praised Mr Bracken 'who had won a name as an authority on historical matters concerning Plymouth' and 'Mr AS Parker, jun., who possessed much of his father's interest and experience in archaeological matters.'

The celebrated Member for Middlesex said that Plymouth's antiquities were a potential asset for benefit of the city in material ways and further that the society had humanitarian as well as historical, archaeological and material considerations in mind. Alluding to the Ancient Monuments Acts (which of course he had been instrumental in steering through Parliament) Sir Philip mentioned 'that 2,500 memorials throughout the country have been registered, and in Devonshire 150. But in Plymouth there has not been a single registration.'

Miss Bayly (whose family have owned the Mayflower 'Island' House for centuries, seconded Sir Philip's proposal for the Old Plymouth Society and said that the city owed him a great debt of gratitude for trying to form the society.

Isaac Foot, who had been born in Notte Street and who was at that time also a sitting MP (for Bodmin), also expressed appreciation for Sir Philip's work and said that Plymouth had never laid sufficient store and emphasis on her very rich history.

'Neglect to safeguard and protect the last vestiges of visible connection between past and present would incur the righteous indignation of the people of the future against those of the present and, perhaps, would render applicable Macaulay's statement "That a people which takes no pride in the achievements of its remote ancestors will never achieve anything worthy to be remembered by its remote descendants"."

No.32 New Street, fully reconditioned.

THE 1930s

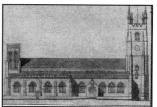
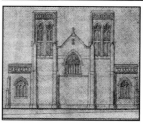

Above: *the ancient Rose and Crown demolished in the 1920s*. Right: *Southcombe Parker's designs for St Andrew's Church.*

Clearly the efforts of all those involved in driving forward the Old Plymouth Fund and then the Old Plymouth Society had done much to prick the local consciousness in respect of one or two of its architectural gems, few of which were as valuable as the so-called Prysten House. As Parker and Bracken were to describe it in their guide to the City's historic remnants, it was: *"Perhaps the most interesting relic of ancient work remaining in Plymouth."*

'Fortunately,' they continued, '*it is being carefully preserved and restored by the Vicar and a Committee in continuance of the scheme inaugurated by the Bishop of Bradford, when Vicar of St Andrew's.*'

What the authors didn't say was that Southcombe Parker himself was directly involved with its restoration, which owed much to his knowledge of local architectural treasures:

'*Father procured joists with identical moulding to those which still remained in the Prysten House from Membland Hall, Newton Ferrers, which was being demolished at that time.*' [Southcombe Parker jnr in a letter written to his daughter, Jill, in 1979]

Neither was it mentioned that the impetus for this restoration was probably tied up with the fact that following the bestowal of City status on Plymouth in 1928, it was thought that St Andrew's Church may in turn have been elevated to Cathedral status and the Prysten House (which Jennifer Barber fairly conclusively demonstrated in 1973 has never been

a priest's house or even, prior to the twentieth century, connected with the church in any direct way) was apparently earmarked to be the 'new' cathedral offices.

In addition to overseeing the restoration of the Prysten House, Southcombe Parker also worked on the adjacent Abbey Hall and, a decade or so later, would come up with a plan which 'would have provided suitable dignity commensurate with the raising of Plymouth to a suffragan bishopric' (EH 2 February 1964). The story goes that one morning in 1942 – the year after St Andrew's had been reduced to a shell by the Lufftwaffe, Southcombe Parker '*awoke and told of a vision that had come to him during the night. His vision was of St Andrew's with a chancel and nave roof raised to allow the insertion of a clerestory and the addition of small twin towers at the east end of the church.*'

To return to the early thirties however, all this work around Abbey Place was of no avail when it came to saving the little row of properties that made up Abbey Place itself. Despite the best efforts of the newly formed Old Plymouth Society, redevelopment was hastening the removal of ancient curios all over the City, and more especially in and around the heart of old Plymouth – the Barbican.

The wonderful old Rose and Crown in Old Town Street had gone a few years earlier and in October 1930 we find a Herald writer (Bracken?) noting how: '*... passing down Treville-street recently I observed a few prominent*

Slate-hung houses in Treville Street on the corner of Green Street, demolished in the late 1930s.

members of the Old Plymouth Society inspecting the outside of two old slate-hung houses at the corner of Green-street.' [where the old Martyn's Gate stood]'

'Of course, the inevitable group of errand boys and children assembled, as they always do if anyone stops to examine the sky or the ground. After a time the members concerned entered the houses – presumably to view the body, in the opinion of the onlookers.'

'These houses are scheduled for demolition. It is a pity, but, judging from the outside, I fear there is no hope. Not being an expert I cannot say whether it will cost more to demolish and remove the houses and carry out the necessary repairs to adjoining property and roadways than to make the houses fit for human habitation. Neglect and decay have gone too far, I think.'

'The moral is that the necessary steps to save these old buildings should have been taken earlier and that it should be the business of any Housing Committee to consider what they can save rather than wait for protests and appeals from without.'

'These houses stood, I expect, before Stuart kings had ceased to rule. You can see from outside now where long casement windows must have been. I expect they were picturesque then. Now they are hovels. They never should have been – and another link passes.'

Reckoned to date from around 1690-1710, by Parker and Bracken, they were among the early casualties recorded as still standing and eminently worthy of interest in their 1930 guide. Referring to the booklet that same month in the *Western Morning News*, Sir Philip Pilditch said that:

'... it is startling to find that there is at present only the briefest reference to Plymouth's ancient treasures in any of the excellent publications, such as guide books, in which The Hoe, Sound, and modern buildings, such as the Guildhall, are set forth – but that lack will now be supplied.'

'What the Society hopes is that the Corporation will refer the matter to a Special Committee, constituted of the members interested in the matter and of the Museum Committee, authorized to examine these things carefully with the officers of the committee of the Old Plymouth Society, and to devise means of exercising the desired protection. A few of them already

belong to the Corporation, which in the past, it is sad, but true, to say, has not always saved them from destruction or desecration. But the major part are still in private hands.'

'In some cases this may be done by an attempt to get the remains scheduled under the Ancient Monuments Act – a Bill to strengthen which I am at this moment endeavouring to get passed in Parliament. Another method is by the instruction of certain officers of the Corporation to examine the buildings, in company with officers of the association, and to report on their condition, ownership, and the best means of preventing them from being destroyed or damaged until the possibility of preserving them has been fully dealt with.'

'The same applies to a regular system of the Corporation's officers reporting to the Museum Committee, in co-operation with the officers of the society, the existence of any ancient fragments of value in buildings threatened with destruction that there may be a chance of acquiring them for the museum.'

He then added ominously: *'During the past year an American agent has purchased, and removed from Plymouth for sale, no doubt at a profit, some 140 such things! At this rate unless something definite is at once set on foot, in a very few years it will be too late, as there will be none left.'*

The comment echoed an earlier remark made by the American Consul, Dr Cooke, at the launch of the Old Plymouth Society at the beginning of the year. Responding to the *'jocular charge that our American cousins are carrying off all our antiquities they can lay hands on,'* Dr Cook retorted *'If you don't want the things … we do.'* Bracken, commenting on the exchange, simply said, *'the moral is clear.'*

Curiously enough, without any regard to a specific anniversary, thought, elsewhere in the City was being given to our relationship with our American cousins, specifically down on the West Pier, near the site of the departure of the Pilgrim Fathers. Here the delightfully different Watch House was about to fall victim to the new road being planned around the front and side of the Citadel. This was a building that Parker and Bracken included in their 1930 guide Plymouth's architectural treasures as being *'a highly interesting and picturesque relic of a port building'*.

Parts of the building were thought to have dated from the mid-late eighteenth century, when it would have stood right on the edge of the natural-stone causey across the entrance to Sutton Pool, but it was substantially erected

The Watch House photographed from different angles and at different times in the years leading up to its demolition in February 1933.

around 1808 not long after Admiral MacBride's east and west piers were laid across the 'causey'. Serving the Police, the Customs and the Tide Survey Office over the years, it was taken down in February 1933.

The following year the Mayflower Memorial was erected just a metre or so from what had been the front door to this building and, having bemoaned its demise, there were those felt that it would have been appropriate perhaps to have incorporated elements of the old Watch House – columns and roofing – into a little covered memorial. Southcombe Parker himself submitted a proposal for the memorial, his vision involved a more traditional Barbican gateway of local stone and allowed a walk-through element more suited to a leaving-point. His idea was, incidentally, eventually executed over 75 years later when the Memorial was revamped for the Millennium. Back in 1934 however the critics' opinions went unheeded: 'however good the design in itself, the material proposed to be used, Portland stone, is alien to the place. The obviously appropriate memorial is some simple thing in local stone, either limestone or granite, the characteristic materials of the Barbican district.' EH May 1934

51 Southside Street, before and after the makeover.

Given this apparent desire to pander to the American connection and, by implication, the tourist market, the decision taken earlier that year with respect to signage on the Barbican seems all the more odd. As the *Evening Herald* reported;

"It must be disheartening to the Old Plymouth Society to find so many of their suggestions turned down, The latest and most inexplicable is to find that a simple request from the Museums Committee (on behalf of the society) to place a direction tablet on a Barbican house indicating the way to No.32 New-street, the restored Elizabethan house, has also been refused. Why, I cannot conceive." WEH 30 Jan 1934

It wasn't all bad news however, and the previous summer the Corporation had executed a reasonable restoration of No.51 Southside Street:

'It is pleasing to see that the character of the old Southside-street house is retained, while the house is at the same time being made habitable. It may not be an exact reproduction of its original Elizabethan front, but we cannot have all we want.' EH 17 June 1933

However as the thirties progressed the appetite for conservation appears to have regressed:- Another house in New Street which: *'had good architectural features and mural paintings,'* came down and new flats were erected. In St Andrew Street the creation of Mumford's new, three-storey garage in 1933 not only saw the obliteration of Abbey Place, but also a large chunk of the very ancient St Andrew Street itself.

Even greater was the loss of a substantial section of High Street. Some of it had only recently been removed when Parker and Bracken published their booklet – viz:

'45 & 46 High Street. Ancient house fronts recently destroyed' and *'48 High Street. "Nichols Court." The side stone walls and arcade in passage, with mullioned windows over, are parts of an Elizabethan large house or mansion. The first two houses in the Court formed its tenement. The main house and front was rebuilt in the 18th century and contained a fine staircase and panelled rooms. All destroyed by the Housing Committee.'*

Within a few years No.44 (*'carcase circa 1600 18th century front. Ship's mast circular stairs'*} and No.50 (*'Queen Anne period'*) and 52, 53 and 54 (also Queen Anne), one with earlier walls, had all gone. And, in their place, came the flats that still stand there today, suggesting that there was a chance that, had the earlier buildings not been demolished to make way for the flats, they may well have survived the Blitz - as indeed did most of the rest of High Street.

The new flats were opened by Viscountess Astor on 10 June 1938. Possessing few redeeming architectural features they did, at least vaguely, preserve the original street line and didn't detract too much from the original building-height line. But it was all part of a brave new

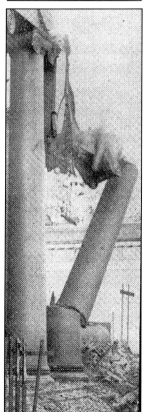

sanitised world, the lines were clean and simple, straight and modern - and by no means unique to Plymouth.

Southcombe Parker senior and junior were unimpressed, as indeed was the younger ASP the previous year when he and Charles Bracken witnessed another act of Corporate vandalism: *'Together we watched the sad sight of the old Theatre Royal being razed to the ground so that a cinema could be built on the site'*. He described the replacement for the building that had brought Plymouth's most influential nineteenth-century architect to the area as being a *'mess of potage'*. Once again that replacement structure survived the War, suggesting that Foulston's impressive 1811 edifice might just have survived the bombing had it been left to stand (although the adjacent, contemporary Georgian buildings, Theatre Royal Hotel and the neighbouring Athenaeum, on the other side, were both burnt out).

The Royal Cinema, as it was originally called, was the third major city-centre cinema to be built that decade (the Gaumont and the Regent were the others and all three seated between 2,300 and 3,500) and along with the celebrated mid-thirties Lido on the Hoe, have been perceived as being a part of a national expression on the part of the younger generation, against the old order, an order *'shattered by the losses of the First World War'* (Michael Pearce: *Saving Time A Review of the Conservation Movement in Britain in the 20th Century*. Publ. in the *Building Conservation Directory* 2000).

This page, left: *Lady Astor opens the new flats built after the properties above were demolished.*
Right, above and below: *the Theatre Royal comes down.*

'Instead of a gradual process of change, many of the younger generation, and the survivors, tended to reject all that had led up to the war in favour of a brave new world. The Modern Movement was cast in concrete. Many of their high-rise flats, cinemas, lidos, zoo buildings, and tube or bus stations are now listed, but many unfashionable Georgian buildings were lost. In defence, the Ancient Monuments Society was formed in 1924, and the Georgian Group in 1937.'

Pearce continues: 'They were encouraged by the architectural historian John Summerson and others in the wake of the redevelopment of Regent Street and the Adelphi, and the threatened loss of Carlton House Terrace in London. In Scotland, extensive slum clearance caused the loss of many attractive vernacular buildings, prompting the Marquess of Bute and others to form the National Trust for Scotland in 1931. The Trust was responsible for the first lists of historic buildings, and through the Little Houses Schemes, at Culross initially, demonstrated that whole areas of historic buildings could be conserved rather than redeveloped.'

Clearly Plymouth's Schedule of Ancient Buildings preceded these Scottish lists by a year or so and this gives us an idea of how, despite the demolitions, Plymouth was nevertheless ahead of the game in certain respects, and, in 1938, curiously enough just a year before the Second World War started, Plymouth Corporation requested an updated version of the 1930 schedule from the Old Plymouth Society. The revision, entitled 'Schedule of Ancient Buildings and Structures in Plymouth whose Preservation as a whole or in part is desirable' was produced by Southcombe Parker and Bracken, with additional assistance from Messrs GW Copeland and E Masson Phillips.

What was most shocking about updating these schedules was not so much the recording of what was still standing as what was not now standing. In less than ten years, since the Old Plymouth Society had produced their first list of 'Ancient Plymouth buildings', no less than thirty properties had been demolished, almost all of them more than two hundred years old and together representing almost a third of all the buildings singled out as being worthy of preservation in 1930. Among them No.28 New Street:

'This particularly interesting building was demolished by the Plymouth Corporation.' [noted Southcombe Parker a few years later] 'It contained a street granite archway and granite Gothic window in the tenement. The upper part was of the William and Mary period – of an exceptionally interesting kind. Probably, there was some sanitary defect, which might perhaps have been rectified, instead demolition was carried out without reference to the Old Plymouth Society Schedule of Ancient Buildings nominated for preservation – no option or reference was given beforehand.'

More depressingly still the number of seventeenth-century buildings lost to the City forever during the 1930s was even greater than the number of seventeenth-century buildings that would be lost in all of the Second World War air raids on Plymouth.

Far left: *Demolished in the thirties - 28 New Street, behind the Island House.*
Right: *Part of the Barbican area, before the War.*

THE SECOND WORLD WAR AND THE 1943 PLAN FOR PLYMOUTH

Above: *St Catherine's Church, Lockyer Street.*
Opposite page: *Barrage Balloon at RAF Mount Batten, looking towards the Barbican*

Although it perhaps seems odd, now with the benefit of hindsight, the advent of war in September 1939 did little to dent the enthusiasm of members of the Old Plymouth Society for their subject and, on a beautiful summer's evening, 12 June 1940, the Society met in Foulston's St Catherine's Church (just across from the Royal Hotel). Led by GW Copeland, the Honorary Secretary, a group of some twenty members met and after a short preliminary address by E Masson Phillips, the Chairman of Committees, Mr Copeland outlined their projected route and its objective *'to highlight late eighteenth and early nineteenth-century elements of Plymouth, with specific regard to Foulston's work'*. The weather was 'brilliant' and the walk informative. Few could have guessed the poignancy of the situation for, before the month was out, Plymouth had recorded its first air-raid alert and within a week of that the first bombs had fallen on the city.

Over the weeks and months that followed, the enemy raids intensified, peaking with the dreadful devastation of March and April 1941 when, in five nights, over a thousand high-explosive bombs and many thousands of incendiaries were dropped on the city. Around 600 civilians lost their lives and over a thousand were injured. It was estimated that 1,500 dwellings were demolished or damaged beyond repair with a further 15,000 badly damaged. Over the whole of the period that the Lufftwaffe were active over Plymouth (July 1940–April 1944) more than 3,750 houses were put beyond reconstruction, while a further 18,000 were seriously damaged, but repairable – of those 'beyond reconstruction' only about 1% were within the Barbican area and of those 'seriously damaged' about .01%, the area had escaped comparatively lightly.

The morning after the night before. Plymouth, 22 March 1941 - note the barrage balloon by the war memorial.

It was in September following those most devastating raids of March and April 1941, forever after referred to as the Blitz of Plymouth, that the Council decided to seek advice from an independent expert. Abercrombie, who was already working on the re-planning of London, was the prime target. However, he may well not have accepted the challenge had not the invitation been personally conveyed to him by Waldorf Astor, *'with whom he shared many pleasant working recollections'* (J Grigg – *Nancy Astor: Portrait of a Pioneer* 1980). Lord Astor who had been appointed as a 'non-political' Lord Mayor at the beginning of the war, invited the respected Town Planner, Patrick Abercrombie, to help put together a plan for the post-war rebuilding of Plymouth.

Born on the banks of the Mersey, Leslie Patrick Abercrombie had been Professor of Civic Design at Liverpool University from 1915-35 when he moved to London to succeed his old Professor at University College. Sixty when the war began he would be commissioned to work on the replanning of several war-torn cities across the country, including London and Kingston upon Hull. The former, written with JH Forshaw, was famously published in 1943, as the Plymouth one was intended to be; the latter, which was produced in conjunction with the celebrated architect Edwin Lutyens, in 1945. In Plymouth, Abercrombie was to work with James Paton Watson, the young Scot who had arrived in Plymouth to take up the post of City Engineer, aged 37, in 1935.

In the meantime Messrs Parker, Copeland, Masson Phillips and Bracken took it upon themselves in November and December 1942 to *'indicate what was then left of the ancient buildings to which reference had been made in previous records.'* By previous records the authors essentially meant the first, 1930 Schedule, because in 1938 they made no mention of buildings that had disappeared off the Historic Area radar. In this survey, which was completed in October 1943, they listed everything that they had provided details of in 1930 and were at pains to discriminate between those buildings that had been completely destroyed by enemy action and those that had been destroyed by local agents or agencies before the War.

Two views from 21 March 1941. Top: the former Mayflower Hotel, on the Barbican. Bottom: Charles Church

Each property in the schedule was coded: 'A' signified that the building had been completely destroyed; 'B' that it had been badly damaged; 'C' that it had been damaged; 'D' that it was intact and 'E', that it had been gutted by fire and its *'fate in some cases is uncertain'*. As noted earlier, the number of seventeenth-century and earlier buildings destroyed between 1930 and 1938 was actually greater than the number destroyed between 1940 and 1943. Overall the lost-building count was slightly higher during the War years (44 as opposed to 39) but that was primarily because the authors listed far more properties in their 1942 schedule than they had in 1930. Doubtless this was partly inspired by the national listing legislation which suggested that listing status could be considered for any building that had been standing prior to 1830 (that is roughly just before the great British period of expansion that came on the back of the Industrial Revolution), placing a whole host of Barbican buildings in the historical searchlight.

Left: *The old part of Plymouth in 1947.*
Above Left: *St Andrew's and the Guildhall 1943.* Right: *Damage to the Prysten House..*

Thus it was that a superficial buildings count suggested that there were just as many buildings in Plymouth worthy of preservation in 1943 as there had been in 1930, but the stark reality was less rosy. In that same time period the City had lost the majority of its truly ancient buildings, one way or another:

'There are three kinds of demolition,' observed Southcombe Parker, when addressing the Plymouth Institution at Sherwell Hall on 3 June 1943:

'1: By the Corporation
2: By Owners
3: By War Damage'

Above: *Charles Church shortly after the War.*
Opposite page, top: *Illustration of Armada Way, Royal Parade axis from 1943 Plan for Plymouth.*
Bottom: *Patrick Abercrombie with Lord Astor.*

'Of these the Corporation is the largest and most reprehensible agent and their work is done without due consideration or enlightenment in any form. Owner's demolitions are done with the purpose of benefiting their pockets and without knowledge of the loss incurred to the City, while the War demolitions are partly necessary for safety but in some cases appear to be part of a concerted effort of clearing everything away for the sake of creating a clean sheet irrespective of whether the buildings are good or sound or not.'

'We all, as children, liked building up towers with bricks or cards for the sheer pleasure of knocking them down again. It seems this instinct is magnified in many grown-ups and that they receive as much pleasure as the children in knocking down ... I was unaware that the instinct could be so strong.'

He concluded: *'It should be clearly understood that the upholders for the retention of Ancient Buildings do not advocate retention where health matters are concerned, or for any reasonable cause – but destruction has been unreasonably large and deplorable'.*

Parker finished his address with that celebrated quote from Macaulay that Isaac Foot had previously invoked:

'A people which take no pride in the noble achievements of its remote ancestors will never achieve anything worthy to be remembered by its remote descendants.'

It is not clear if the Council again provided the impetus for the Old Plymouth Society's 1942/43 revision (as they did in 1938), but with Lord Astor at the helm it is quite likely, and certainly from the wording of a later (1956) revision, it would appear that the authors were privy to the then as yet unpublished 'Plan For Plymouth 1943', which eventually saw light of day in 1944:

'In view of the radical re-planning scheme which the destruction of so much property of all kinds and thoroughfares had virtually made necessary and desirable, it was fully appreciated by the Old Plymouth Society that much of what they had recommended for preservation might have to be removed, or that it was at least threatened with demolition in the not too distant future.'

It was not a statement laced with optimism and the failure of the Society's attempt, following a resolution passed at their July meeting in 1943 to save Outlands House, the birthplace of Robert Falcon Scott, could only have added to the air of resignation.

However although the main thrust of the 1943 Plan For Plymouth was a fabulous new City Centre for Plymouth (Devonport and Stonehouse were very much the poor relations in this bold new vision), it did, in the words of Lord Astor, writing from the Lord Mayor's Parlour (No.2 Elliot Terrace): 'no violence to historic Plymouth'. More than that, this was 'our chance to repair past errors in lay-out and to create a new Plymouth worthy both of its fame and its site between the hills and the water.'

THE BARBICAN OF TO-DAY VIEWED FROM THE EAST

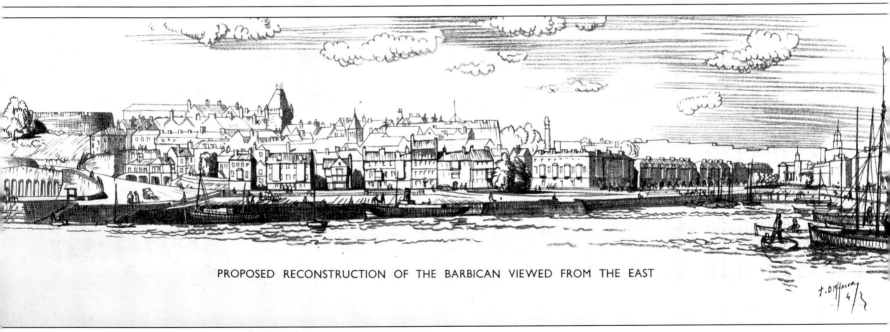

PROPOSED RECONSTRUCTION OF THE BARBICAN VIEWED FROM THE EAST

Illustrations from the 1943 Plan for Plymouth

The opening chapter of the 150-page case-bound volume was even entitled *Historic Plymouth*, giving the reader the at-a-glance impression that this part of the city, which had substantially escaped major damage, was due to be polished and cherished.

'Old Plymouth, miraculously escaped from destruction, is treated quite distinctly from the modern Centre, which has invaded its ancient precinct in order to include St Andrew's Church. The Old Town, carefully renovated and reconditioned, but without archaeological faking, looks towards it's own original Sutton Harbour. This marked and intentional apposition of the historic town, close to, but distinct from and contrasted with the modern City Centre and commercial area, will form one of the characteristic features of the Plymouth of the future. In so many towns the historic centre has grown into the modern centre and become effaced through repeated rebuildings: here old and modern stand side by side, each possessing its special quality.'

It sounded promising to the ears of the conservationists and to those of the overseas tourists as represented by the Hon. John G Winant, his excellency the American Ambassador to the Court of St James, who wrote the foreword to The Plan.

'Generations of voyaging Americans, landing at Plymouth, have found a crowded, prosperous place in a superb scenic setting. They saw the old town of Pilgrim days ... if the streets were sometimes curving and narrow, if the layout was sometimes picturesque rather than convenient, my countrymen expected that and were delighted by it.'

Indeed. As the authors of The Plan explained: 'Although the ancient city wall via Hoe Gate, Frankfort Gate, Old Town Gate and Gasking Gate, contained within its perimeter a larger area, the smaller central area of some 40 to 50 acres, bounded by the Hoe, Old Town Street and Treville Street, contains the greater part of the remaining historic buildings; while its centre, the Barbican, still retains, in addition to many buildings, the old street pattern of narrow cobbled streets which existed in the time of our famous Elizabethan sea-captains and was at a later date traversed by the Pilgrim Fathers on their embarkation to the Americas.'

'We consider that within this small district there is an area worthy of preservation from every point of view, and we recommend intensification of effort towards the reconditioning and reconstruction of the buildings

so that, whilst retaining its historic features of narrow roads, winding, step-crossed lanes, enclosed courts and tiered houses, it shall possess those additional communal and personal facilities demanded by modern standards of living.'

'We do not suggest for one moment that a faked, exhibitionist pseudo antique district should be created, but that this comparatively small area of the city – its historic precinct – should be set aside for special attention, its remaining ancient buildings and streets carefully restored, and the whole area controlled and directed in its future re-development, so as to form a fitting frame for the priceless antiquities which it contains.'

The authors went on to quote 'the enthusiastic historian, Sir Philip Pilditch' repeating the line from the Elizabethan Plymouth pamphlet to which we have already referred, but which bears repeating:

'If it were anywhere on the Riviera or Provence, or in Spain, or Italy, English and American tourists would be found going into raptures over it, but here it is in drab old England and we have not known how to make the most of it.'

Returning to the main text of The Plan, we read; 'Interest in this national historic heritage is vividly portrayed by many of the present visitors from overseas who, by the fortunes of war, are now among us and who, having seen the spots where their forefathers landed on the other side, exhibit a lively and intense interest in the Barbican and its Mayflower Stone. Some of them ['them' being a veiled reference to the American servicemen stationed in Plymouth as part of the build up to the Normandy Invasion – which was of course still all shrouded in secrecy] having seen Williamsburg, the reconstructed historical piece on the other side of the Atlantic, express their surprise and wonderment that similar steps have not been taken to preserve and enshrine the yet more personally intimate and historic relics here. The right effect in old Plymouth would be obtained by the use of vernacular building and materials, without any strong stylistic bias.'

'Although the neighbourhood has been allowed to decay, so much of the shape and atmosphere of antiquity still remains as to make its rehabilitation both practical and worth-while, and we support and commend the process of reconditioning on which the Council had embarked prior to the war, as opposed to any process of clearance; and we further suggest that external restoration be made to accompany this internal reconditioning.'

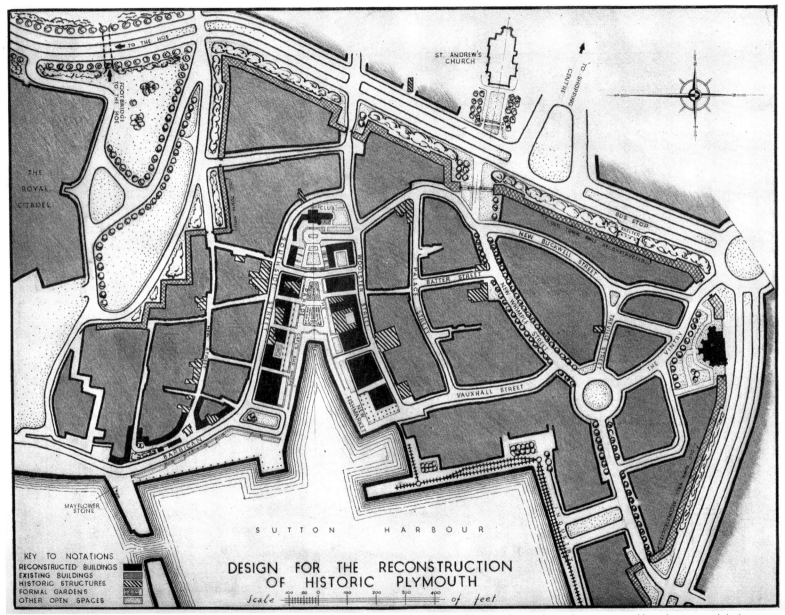

DESIGN FOR THE RECONSTRUCTION OF HISTORIC PLYMOUTH

KEY TO NOTATIONS
RECONSTRUCTED BUILDINGS
EXISTING BUILDINGS
HISTORIC STRUCTURES
FORMAL GARDENS
OTHER OPEN SPACES

Scale 100 50 0 100 200 300 400 of feet

The proposals for the Barbican published in the 1943 Plan note how little of the Barbican, north and west of the Parade was destined to survive, and how the proposed dual carriageway would have isolated 'Historic Plymouth' from the City Centre.

It all sounded marvellous, but the devil was in the detail: *'The Plate facing page 14 shows the ancient district and the effect of war, with the possibilities so revealed; and facing page 13 is a reproduced plan showing our proposals for the future of what may be termed an 'historic precinct'; contrasting sketches of the Barbican waterfront before and after reconditioning, which graphically illustrate the trend of proposals, are also shown.'*

At first glance there undoubtedly appeared to be a healthy chunk of Plymouth's past being preserved in sketches and plans – in marked contrast of course to the treatment of the City Centre, however, closer inspection gave numerous grounds for concern.

For a start there was a major new dual-carriageway severing all the links that the old town had with its ancient parish church – although there did appear to be a pedestrian underpass between the back of the church and some point near the top of High Street. But St Andrew Street was obliterated, apart from one building, No.33, which happily is still standing today. However, gone was the Abbey Hotel, gone the block alongside it on the corner of Whimple Street and gone too was that throroughfare, to be replaced by some odd-looking, all-new New Whimple Street to the east of its earlier namesake, which: *'forms an adequately designed link between the old town and its mother church, St Andrew's, and, incidentally, is more in sympathy with the topographical features of the ground than Howe Street and Looe Street which should disappear.'*

Looe Street ... disappear? Why? Was this not one of the thoroughfares identified 25 years earlier as possessing a number of fine old buildings? Wasn't it also one of the City's oldest streets and one in which Drake himself had had property, and literary and cultural groups had met, it being in the direct line of sight of Plymouth's earlier Guildhalls (from the dawn of the 1600s through to the early 1870s? And were not the late-nineteenth century Council flats which lined one side still eminently habitable, along with those similarly dated and constructed properties either side of the cobbled highway in Howe Street?

And what about Breton Side and the old buildings there? What was the purpose in creating a new street called 'The Vintry' at the expense of the early seventeenth-century King's Head and its mixed bag of neighbours? As for any new thoroughfare being 'more in sympathy with the topographical features of the ground' how does that fit in with preserving the old street pattern?

It was all starting to sound exactly like the ghastly mess the authors were at pains to say they were anxious to avoid, namely a *'faked, exhibitionist pseudo antique district'.* The warning bells should have started ringing when they spoke of *'a wine store which has been built of recent years nearby,'* which *'illustrates the sort of treatment that we have in mind.'*

Having not acknowledged the Looe Street/Whimple Street junction as the very heart of the old town – prior to the building of the Jacobean Guildhall here the market cross had been on that site – they turned their attention to: *'...the heart of this (historic) precinct – the Parade and the Barbican; ... and for this small area we make definite proposals as to reconstruction, intended not only to make good the damage caused by enemy action and the ravages of time but to create, in addition, a centre of interest for townsman and visitor alike by replacing the somewhat dull and dingy character of the present buildings with something more in keeping with the spirit of the past.'*

Note, re-creation not in keeping with each particular property's past but *'more in keeping with the spirit of the past'.* Doesn't that sound remarkably like 'pseudo antique'? But wait, what is this? On cleared space at the west end of the Parade we read of a garden court feature to be introduced: *'terminating in a large enclosure and a club forming a community centre, this combining residential buildings, gardens and a seamen's club. Such a centre would be the modern counterpart of the medieval town square and would go far towards improving the locality as a centre of local life.'*

Hawker's Avenue: *'a wine store which has been built of recent years nearby,'* which *'illustrates the sort of treatment that we have in mind.'*
Top: *Before.* Bottom: *After 1937.*

On cleared space at the west end of the Parade we read of a garden court feature to be introduced 'terminating in a large enclosure and a club forming a community centre, this combining residential buildings, gardens and a seamen's club. Such a centre would be the modern counterpart of the medieval town square and would go far towards improving the locality as a centre of local life.'

All that despite the fact that in an earlier mission statement the authors had chosen to remove the Fish Market to a less obtrusive site and to demolish the old Fish Market building in the process.

Overall, however, in the context of what was being proposed for the City Centre it was a considerable concession: in a conservational context though it was worrying. Nevertheless, when the 1943 Plan was eventually published, in April 1944, it was the 'Design for the Reconstruction of Historic Plymouth' that stole the front page picture slot, with the more iconic visions for the City Centre being relegated, along with the model and its mentors, to the inside pages. It was there we also found the somewhat prescient editorial:

'Now revealed to a waiting world, 'A Plan for Plymouth' is so comprehensive as to demand the most careful consideration. Not lightly can the shape of places and things which will affect posterity be resolved upon. There will be much discussion and, without doubt, it will continue for years.'

The *Western Morning News* published earlier that same Thursday, concentrated on the civic and shopping centres and was a little more spikey in its approach. After referring to the many 'delays and disappointments' the editor informed his readership that:

'The whole Report could have been in the hands of citizens many months ere this. The Western Morning News offered to publish it in its columns as soon as it was available, but for reasons which are still obscure to us this offer was refused. We have always considered that the Report should receive the fullest possible publicity at the earliest moments, so that the citizens of Plymouth should have every possible opportunity of discussing its contents, for criticizing and for suggesting alternatives. We have never agreed with the attitude of mind which seems to consider that this plan for the future of Plymouth should be treated with the secrecy which of necessity surrounds the design of a new warplane.'

Having got that off his chest however a more conciliatory tone was adopted; 'The Lord Mayor and the members of the Council are to be congratulated on their vision in having these plans prepared, and thanks are due in large measure to the Lord Mayor for securing the services of such an eminent expert as Professor ABERCROMBIE. No doubt the plans as visualised at present will have to be greatly changed in detail to meet the practical

working conditions of the city and the overriding question of finance will have to be continuously kept in view.'

Responding to a question at a Luncheon held in the British Restaurant at the Guildhall (hosted by the Lord Mayor, Lord Astor), to launch the report, Paton Watson stated that: 'it was anticipated that the business centre of the city could be reinstated and fully going within five years, but the Ministry of Town and Country Planning gave an ultimate period of twelve years for completion of a scheme of such magnitude.'

Lord Astor, Lord Mayor of Plymouth, addressing guests of Plymouth Corporation at luncheon in the British Restaurant, at the Guildhall, after their inspection of models of Plymouth reconstruction plans.

Asked whether there would not be a greater speeding up if they used the existing streets and tried to improve them Mr Watson said: 'That is quite impossible, you would have to widen the existing streets and that would leave you insufficient depth to develop and recreate all the traffic horrors which we want to obviate. Something better should have been done in the past.'

Putting the whole Plan into some sort of perspective, we read that the proposals were intended to cover a period of many years, but that the authors put the plan of reconstruction into two periods, taking into account of course, the prevailing circumstances – we were still at war.

'The first period would be:
1.	Roads, sewers, and public utilities.
2.	Housing and schools.
3.	Reinstatement of industry and shopping.
4.	City Centre.

The priorities for the second period should be:-
1.	Housing and reconstruction areas.
2.	Main communications and new roads.
3.	Hotels and boarding houses.
4.	Cultural area.
5.	Historic Plymouth.
6.	Theatres and kinemas.
7.	Open spaces, parks and parkways.'

The Old Plymouth Society in the Prysten House. Roger Serpell addresses the meeting from the floor. Ted Masson Phillips, the vicar of St Andrews and Gustav Gopeland at the committee table.

POST WAR BLUES . . . AND REDS
THE POLITICS OF PRESERVATION

Placed ninth in the pecking order, it certainly didn't seem likely that anything was going to happen overnight in and around the Barbican area, and, shortly after the war (November 1946), the members of the Old Plymouth Society felt impelled to request the City Council to continue its help and co-operation in the protection of Ancient Monuments of Plymouth, and to secure the active interest of the City Engineer and his Officers, with this end in view.'

Abercrombie, the man who had, incidentally, been instrumental in setting up and publicizing the Council for the Preservation of Rural England, back in 1926 – he was the first Honorary Secretary – was increasingly a background figure as regards the implementation of 'The Plan'. Meanwhile other towns and cities were producing their own proposals, not all of which, it has to be said, were as sympathetic to their heritage as Plymouth's Plan purported to be. Coventry for example, which had lost *acres of its oldest, most evocative lanes'* (Robert Gill: *Relocating Medieval Coventry*) in a major redevelopment in the mid-late 1930s, talked about relocating 'in the few cases where old buildings are disturbed' (*Future Coventry: 1945*): while Newcastle's City Centre Plan, published that same year and masterminded by their City Engineer and Planning Officer, Percy Parr,

spoke of how 'prosperity after the war will depend to a large extent upon roads and road transport, and every effort should be made to improve these vital communications and expedite the flow of traffic, which too often is impeded by obstructive narrow roads and bad surfaces.' The report throughout treated conservation as a matter of picturesque features and limited it to proposals consistent with the economic development of the city, preserving only the more important ancient or historic buildings. It even recommended demolishing surrounding townscape to reveal such buildings.

Plymouth of course was fortunate in that the prosperity of the city was no longer dependent on development in and around its historic quarter. Because of the unique way the town/city had evolved, the old part had been rather left behind and, even more fortuitously, had largely escaped the worst ravages of the aerial bombardment. It was also happily blessed with one of the country's more advanced conservation-based societies.

Generally speaking, across the country 'Conservation' was still very much in its infancy; major encouragement had been given to this process with the ordering of a survey of the nation's building-stock, a process which began in 1947 and which was partly in response to the losses sustained during the war. Early in the conflict, in 1941, after many major towns and cities had already suffered from aerial bombing, the National Buildings Record was created to record the architectural heritage which was under threat and in 1944 the Town and Country Planning Act of 1944 was passed through Parliament. This marked the setting up of a system for identifying buildings of architectural or historical importance, hopefully to prevent their wilful destruction in the rebuilding process. However, although the Act introduced the concept of 'listing' it didn't actually do much more than assist in the identification process.

Clearly though, it was a step in the right direction, much as the international initiative taken at Athens had been in 1931, when there was a declaration for the protection of cultural monuments throughout the world, more legislation was needed before 'listing' could have a significant impact. There also needed to be a greater awareness of our national and local heritage and no one man did more to make England aware of its treasurers than the son of a German-born Jewish merchant from Leipzig, Nikolaus Pevsner.

Pevsner came to England as a thirty-year-old art history lecturer in 1934. He came to escape the Nazi threat and taught at the universities of Birmingham, London, Oxford and Cambridge.

An early, active member of the Georgian Group, which had been founded in 1937, Pevsner, as an academic, and an interested outsider, quickly realised that the study of architectural history had little status among England's ivory towers and he came up with the idea of writing a series of comprehensive county guides listing each area's particular treasurers.

He floated the idea to Allen Lane, the former Bristol Grammar School pupil who was the same age as Pevsner and who had conceived the idea of the contemporary quality paperback novel in 1934. Lane had been travelling back from Devon to London after visiting Agatha Christie, when he had scoured Exeter Station searching for something to read. Already involved in the literary industry, Lane envisaged setting up a publishing house to produce paperbacks that could be sold at sixpence a time (then the same price as a packet of cigarettes) via a vending machine, which was quickly dubbed a 'Penguincubator'. It was Lane's secretary who had suggested the name Penguin as a 'dignified but flippant' name for the company.

In 1943 Penguin had published Pevsner's *Outline of European Architecture* and Lane not only warmed to Pevsner's idea of the 'County' series, he even employed two part-time assistants, both of them German refugee art historians, to help gather the basic information. Work began on the series in 1945 and in 1951, the first volume, on Cornwall, hit the bookstalls. Devon, published as two volumes – North and South – followed in 1952.

Right from the beginning it was realised that Pevsner was creating an inventory of such importance that *'so far as architecture is concerned, will relegate most other guides to the status of picture books.'* (*The Architect's Journal*).

Plymouth occupied around twenty of Pevsner's 350-odd pages on the south of the county and his opening remarks provided a neat snapshot of where we were at, at the dawn of the 1950s:

'Plymouth, with just over 200,000 inhabitants, is the largest city in Devon – in fact, the only large city in Devon. It is also one of the worst war-damaged cities in Britain, and so, at the time of writing, its centre is not a picture to be described in terms of architecture, but of dust or mud and rubble and weirdly shaped fragments of walls. This novel setting helps a few of the remaining buildings (eg the Guildhall) but denies Plymouth that urban individuality which Stonehouse and Devonport have been fortunate enough to preserve.'

Plymouth 1949. Royal Parade and Armada Way are laid out .

'Yet this much can still be said. Plymouth makes one realise how peaceable the architecture of England is. It is the only British city whose existence appears to be centred on war. With Naval Dockyard and Naval Hospital, Victualling Yard and Citadel, Marine Barracks and Raglan Barracks, and the chain of forts around, nearly all its principal accents are naval or military.'

The author then went on to itemise the various churches, public buildings and service institutions around the Three Towns and then started a six-page section headed 'perambulations' with a thumbnail sketch of the surviving bits of Plymouth that date *'from the Middle Ages to the seventeenth century'*.

Inevitably this was almost entirely that area we now call the Barbican, and in his roll call Pevsner lists many buildings singled out by Southcombe Parker and all who'd followed him (GW Copeland was one of the first to be mentioned in Pevsner's foreword), a number of which were already living on borrowed time. Pevsner and his wife had done their Devon groundwork in 1949, before any of the new city-centre buildings had been completed, and indeed before the vast majority had even been started and also when No.6 Norley Street (the former Charles Church Vicarage), the neighbouring Household of Faith in Vennell Street and most of High Street, were still standing.

Aware of the danger so much of our heritage was in, the same year that Pevsner was putting the finishing touches to 'South Devon' an architect working in the City Architect's office, Mr Z Bienawski he was 'entrusted with the task of preparing a comprehensive report on the ancient part of the City.' As an architect Mr Bienawski said that he *'could not fail to be attracted by the charm of the Old City,'* soon after his arrival in Plymouth *'several years ago'* (he was writing in 1954). His report, was one of the most detailed that has ever been undertaken of the area: street by street, it detailed every house, every business, every pub, shop and café; it tabulated how many of the properties were *'fit, unfit, sub-standard, occupied and already unoccupied'*. It looked at the population distribution, the employment situation, the fishing industry and examined the viability of the area as it presently stood and with different options regarding its future.

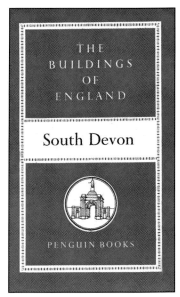

One of these options was: *'To throw overboard all sentiments for history and tradition, and to modernise the area to meet purely economical and housing needs of New Plymouth'* the other *'to rehabilitate the old City with enlightened respect to her history and her characteristic Town Scape, yet in conformity with contemporary standards of living so that she may pursue her sound traditional life AND attract visitors and win their affection.'*

Bienawski's introduction was clear in its preferred option as he stated that his report *'intends to induce the Civic Authorities to move one or two paces towards the enlightened reconstruction of one of the most precious parts of the City.'*

Sadly, however, having commissioned the document, the City did little with it, just as they hadn't apparently done anything with the report they had commissioned from the Royal Society for the Protection of Ancient Buildings three years earlier: *'This proposed clearing out the valueless buildings and restoring old. It is still in the pigeon holes.'* (Crispin Gill – *Plymouth Barbican Revived*, 1995).

As all these surveys were being done Pevsner's muddy, dusty canvas was changing on a daily basis and although the 1943 Plan had been an elaborate, and widely publicised document (which still changes hands for considerably more than it cost when first published) and although it had been the main template for post-war redevelopment, it was by no means set in stone. In 1952 a new document, 'The Plymouth Development Plan' was unveiled. If Bienawski's survey had been a part of the background research for this plan there is little evidence that his hopes for moving 'the Civic Authorities one or two paces towards the enlightened reconstruction' had been successful.

The document acknowledged that the area: *'probably assumed its present general outline in the XVth Century or even earlier'* and that *'there has been little if any change in the street pattern since before the time of Sir Francis Drake, and some of the buildings of those days still remain.'*

It also observed that *'... on some counts it might be said that the area is badly laid out ... but the plan fits snugly into the location, there are no awkward traffic junctions , and the design of the Parade, around the western arm of Sutton Harbour, has that intimate charm which seems no longer to form part of the townplanner's art.'*

However, and more significantly, the townplanner's art did now deem other aspects of Historic Plymouth less acceptable: *'The main criticism against the general layout valid by modern standards is the width of the streets, which are mostly too narrow to afford proper light and ventilation to the tall buildings which line them, and are certainly inadequate for the needs of modern transport.'*

'Valid by modern standards,' what exactly does that mean? Weren't these buildings put in place several centuries before the introduction of gas lighting and the discovery of electricity? Were they unacceptable then? And remember, when reference is made to *'tall buildings'* here, we are talking three or four stories at the most, not tall by the 'modern standards' of the twenty-first century. Ask any of the visitors who make York one of the most successful tourist honeypots in modern Britain what they like about that historic city and they will almost certainly cite the narrow streets. Plymouth still has a few, but in 1952 it had several more, and the Development Plan of that year spoke very much with a forked tongue when it made reference to its heritage.

Paragraphs 664-71 on page 96 of this new 'Development Plan' were of greatest interest for the Barbican – or 'Neighbourhood Area No.18' as it had become;

'664. This area, Historic Plymouth, is one of the main sightseeing attractions of Plymouth, and it is essential that it shall be maintained, not as a museum piece, but as a living entity justifying its continued existence.'

It is the expression *'justifying its continued existence'* that set the first wave of alarm bells ringing.

'665. The section north of Woolster Street, where some clearance has followed war damage, is included in the Central Areas of Comprehensive Development. Apart from the south side of Looe Street, the former character of this section has been largely lost, and it is proposed to erect houses designed in harmony with the associations of the area.'

This was local authority speak for *'we've demolished just about everything that the Germans left standing between the back of Looe Street and Woolster Street (Vauxhall St) and we're going to build new flats here that are vaguely in line with the old street layout.'*

In fairness this area had not been the richest source of Plymouth's ancient architectural gems, but this was only the beginning:

Above: *Lower Batter Street looking north.* Top right: *Upper Batter Street looking south.* Right: *Stillman Street.*

Top: *Hick's Lane off Looe Street, with entrance to Looe Place first on left.*
Below: *Looe Place. All cleared to make way for new housing.*

'666. South of Woolster Street, around the Parade and the Barbican, a number of Elizabethan buildings are still in use, and the section as a whole retains a great deal of its original character. Every effort will be made to ensure that it continues to do so. The houses lining the narrow streets should be renovated and brought up to modern standards as far as possible. Additional light and air should be admitted to them by clearing away the clutter of small dwellings in the congested courts between the streets. Some of these courts, such as Camber's Court, have a quaint picturesqueness which sentimentality would preserve, but such action would not be in the best interest of the area as a whole. The cottages in the courts should go, and their sites should be adapted as gardens for the houses fronting the streets, so that these may house satisfactorily a reasonable quota of workers who must of necessity live in this area.'

Again the key phrase here was *'which sentimentality would preserve, but such action would not be in the best interest of the area as a whole'* - according to whom, exactly?

Among the proposals in the next few paragraphs we read that *'a new service lane could well be laid out between Southside Street and New Street'* (667), that *'St Saviour's Church, on Lambhay Hill should be reinstated'* (668), and that *'the small school in Castle Street could be adapted as a nursery school'* (669).

'The community centre at the west end of the Parade' (a legacy of the 1943 Plan) was still on the list of proposed innovations while paragraph 671 grudgingly acknowledged that the Barbican did have *'special characteristics'*;

'Warehouses and other commercial premises bordering on the quays of Sutton Pool, the fish market at the Barbican, a distillery, bonded stores, and small factories all provide employment, and contribute to the peculiar charm which this corner of Plymouth has for visitors.'

Clearly the implication here was that the authors of the 1952 Development Plan themselves did not quite get this 'peculiar charm' themselves. It would also appear that this 1952 Plan had nothing like the circulation or exposure of it's wartime precursor, as a letter from the Chamber of Commerce to Town Clerk makes perfectly obvious:

9 June 1954. Re: Housing in the Barbican Area: *'I have to refer to a memorandum addressed to you in July 1952, with reference to the above. At that time, the Chamber of Commerce was concerned about the proposal to erect Flats in the Barbican Area. It will be remembered that the 'Plan for Plymouth' envisaged the retention of this area as an Historic Precinct. Indeed at one time it was proposed to convert the area into a walled neighbourhood.'*

'While the Chamber recognises the need for housing near the Barbican, and that reconditioning of some insanitary buildings is necessary, we are anxious that nothing should be erected to destroy the appearance of this historic precinct. At the time this was discussed, we understood that the City Architect was preparing a plan for the future of the Barbican Area, and we were assured that every endeavour would be made to retain as much as possible of the association with the past.'

'Would it be possible for the City Architect to make public his proposals for this area, as he has done with the Civic Centre? This would perhaps allay the fears of a large body of the public who imagine that the whole area is to be destroyed and replaced with blocks of Flats entirely out of keeping with Plymouth's historic precinct.'

The Town Clerk's reply was somewhat curt: *'Your letter of the 9th instant was mentioned at the last meeting of the Reconstruction Committee when they were considering a report on the Sutton Harbour and Cattewater Areas.'*

'The policy of the Council with regard to the Barbican Area has been made public, and I am desired by the Committee to inform you that this policy remains unchanged. The Housing Committee are very alive to the necessity of keeping and, if possible, restoring the character of the historic precinct.'

This ultimately unhelpful reply would have been frustrating enough for a member of the public, one might have thought that the Chamber would have been offered a more satisfactory answer. Chamber secretary, H Michell, clearly thought so, and having thanked the Town Clerk for his missive he went on to write: *'As this* [policy] *statement appears to have escaped my notice, would you please be good enough to let me know wherein this policy has been published.'*

The succinct reply to this latest correspondence simply referred the Secretary to paragraphs 664-73 of the Development Plan and two minutes of the Reconstruction Committee (from December 1952 and March 1953).

By September the Chamber had not only acquainted themselves with the 1952 Plan they had also made contact with Mr Bienawski and, on Thursday 2 September 1954, two leading Chamber members, CP Brown and CJ Woodrow, met Mr Bienawski at the latter's business premises – Blight & White – in Prince Rock.

At the meeting various specific parts of the Barbican were mentioned, including the very vulnerable areas of Lambhay Hill and Castle Street *'where there was a building now used as storage space for fish boxes, etc., which is capable of being converted into a Repertory Theatre'* and New Street which had *'many interesting houses worth preserving'*. *'The narrow lanes … a feature of the period of the building of the area'* should also be retained.

Looking up Castle Street.

Mr Bienawski made the point that the 1947 Act: '… lists buildings and houses, as well as churches, which are of historical interest, and imposes some obligations on local authorities, but it does not seem to give them the authority to compel the owners of such properties to do anything against their wishes. An individual owner of any scheduled property cannot make alterations to it without notifying the Local Authority. On the other hand, if permission was refused and the owner went to Law, he might win the case. No Local Authority could compel a private owner to behave in any particular way.' Furthermore, he added: 'much of the property would cost a good deal of money to put into a habitable state.'

The problem was that the Housing Committee were desperate to re-house as many people as they could as quickly as they could. Mr Bienawski said that he knew that plans were afoot for part of the area and that modern houses would be quite out of keeping. He also said he was quite happy for Mr Brown to use his Barbican report and all the maps and tables that went with it and that he would prepare a précis of the document for the Chamber's use.

When the Chamber later met to discuss the way forward, Mr Brown had a complete copy of the Bienawski report and there was a suggestion made that prior to this the only person who had read the document was WA 'Darkie' Miller, the Chairman of the Housing Committee.

The grandson of a freed slave, Miller had first been elected to the Council in 1925 and so devoted was he to the task of re-housing Plymouth's war-weary population that he had refused the Lord Mayoralty in 1947. As far as the Chamber were concerned, on the issue of Plymouth's historic Barbican, it was agreed that Miller and his Conservative counterpart, Harold Pattinson, 'had no regard for the city, nor do they see that the Barbican area is to a large extent the bread and butter of Plymouth in its attraction to visitors, which should be obvious to anyone who had the interest of Plymouth at heart.'

Above all the Chamber members felt that 'the Barbican Area could not be treated as an ordinary housing area.'

With all this in mind a three-man deputation of the Chamber – CP Brown, CJ Woodrow and Leslie Paul - was given a hearing at the meeting of the Reconstruction Committee on Monday, 18 October 1954.

'Our sole desire is to be helpful to the Reconstruction Committee and the City Council in the very difficult problem that faces them,' said spokesman Brown, who, after outlining their passion as Plymothians and the historic significance of the city asked for 'certain steps to gain the ends that we all have in mind be set in motion forthwith:

Firstly; that an immediate standstill order be made on any reconstruction in the area known as the Barbican.

Secondly; that an independent architect, well versed in all matters concerning the preservation of historic precincts be employed to make a fresh survey of the area and recommendations for its treatment.

And thirdly; based on this information a definite policy be laid down for well-governed and strict control of all building and road-making in this area now and in the future, so that everything that is done, shall be done with a view to preserving this district as an historic precinct.'

'The reason for the first request is that during the post-war years, and even quite recently, piecemeal construction has been going on, doubtless in accordance with the by-laws, but without due regard to the historic nature of the district, and this it is still going on or in contemplation and that unless checked at once, irreparable damage may be done and the historic atmosphere of the place is destroyed for all time.'

The Town Clerk, S Lloyd Jones, subsequently wrote thanking the delegation for their visit and was at pains to point out that the Council had invited the Society for the Protection of Ancient Buildings to the City in 1948 and that their report had recognised the Barbican as 'one of the main sight-seeing attractions at Plymouth'. The letter however did little more than pay lip service to the concept of conservation and made it quite clear that 'it is the intention of the Council that the block of property bounded by Woolster Street, High Street, the Parade and Lower Batter Street, shall be further cleared and used for housing and the provision of some shops … elevations will conform with the elevation of buildings in the vicinity and for facing in local material.'

The Chamber was not impressed and they were right not to be. The shops didn't materialise and their conclusion that 'the historic precinct is to be treated as a residential area, as the committee seems to think only in terms of dwelling houses,' appeared to be well founded.

Three views of the erstwhile bottom section of High Street, all cleared to make way for new flats. Note the JL Nash building, or part of it, is on the left of all three images.

'This is surely not what one would expect to amount to rehabilitation of our historic city,' they opined, 'this bit of narrow policy is already practically and disastrously illustrated by four specimens of housing accommodation within this area, viz. Corporation flats in Upper New Street; two blocks on Lower Lambhay Hill, and a block of flats submerged in the gloom of the old Jewish cemetery.'

However, it wasn't just flats that were being built; a 'Précis on the Barbican Area' produced around this time noted that:

'...not only are the characteristic old buildings decaying, but crude adaptations, carried out indiscriminately, do more harm than the tooth of time, viz.; the warehouse in New Street close to the Elizabethan House, or a new atrocious store (Dingle's Bacon Curing Plant) in Friars Lane close to the exceptionally fine Trinity House.'

As 1955 dawned, however, little progress appeared to have been made - in April the *Western Morning News* reported:

'Mr Paton Watson said that he and the City Architect were being pressed morning and night for a plan for the Barbican, but it was difficult to plan when the main buildings of the area were built 500 years ago, where the slope was one in two, and where the Medical Officer was anxious to condemn many of the buildings which, if pulled down, would make most of the others fall down.'

The report continued: 'Now the Fine Art Commission was interested and he and the City Architect were interested to see what these long-haired gentlemen would suggest.'

'We are as enthusiastic as anyone that it should be preserved in its character and use, but it is a difficult job and one that will take time.'

Exactly two months later the same paper announced that the City Council were seeking Compulsory Purchase Orders for two areas of the Barbican;

Top left: *South-eastern block of High Street.* Bottom left; *Friar's Lane with Trinity House and part of the new Dingle's Bacon Curing Plant.*

Barbican c1949, note Castle Street and Lambhay Hill stand proud along with the infill buildings at the back of New Street and to the west of Pin Lane

'The Council wants the Ministry of Housing to confirm orders applying to the block bounded by High-street, Palace-street, and Batter-street, with the exception of the Kitto Institute, Allenby Arms and a printing works. Another concerns two houses in Vauxhall-street.'

'In all, the Council plans to demolish 24 dwellings and an annexe to a bonded warehouse. The Deputy Town Clerk, Mr HR Haydon, said the houses affected in the Barbican were unfit for human habitation. Demolition was the most satisfactory way of dealing with them.'

Mr Haydon said: 'The Port of Plymouth Chamber of Commerce had lodged a general objection on the properties as a whole, and had referred to the historical character of the area. The Chamber was going further than it ought to go. It did not own any property in the area, and it was not one of those who received an invitation to attend the inquiry.'

Mr Woollcombe, answering on behalf of the Chamber, replied that the invitation had come from the Minister of Housing himself.

In the discussions that followed it emerged that no plans had been prepared to show there was a need to acquire the properties and that, furthermore, according to PC Stedman, a surveyor present, £4,500 had been spent on the threatened annexe in the previous four years, with the approval of the local authority.

In conclusion the Chamber objected to a piecemeal development of the area before an overall plan had been presented and while they were not competent to prepare a report of their own, they felt that they were entitled to ask that 'Compulsory Purchase Orders should not be granted until the Minister was satisfied that the Council had an overall plan.'

It further emerged, however, that the report the Council had received from the Society for the Protection of Ancient Buildings, seven years earlier, had pretty much just been filed away.

The following month, on 6 July 1955, the two representatives of the Royal Fine Art Commission visited the Barbican - the secretary Godfrey Samuel and an architect, Louis de Soissons (whose firm had an office in Plymouth after the war and were responsible for one of the more prevalent designs of post-war housing in the area). With them on that visit were the Town

Above left: Bottom of High Street. Below left: 46-51 Palace Street.

82

Top; *Two views of Notte Street, including the buildings refashioned in the 1890s.*
Below: *Corner of Palace Street and High Street.* Middle: *Plymouth Printers, Woolster Street.* Far right: *The Allenby Arms*

Clerk, Lloyd Jones, City Engineer, Paton Watson and the City Architect, HJW Stirling. During the tour they met Eric Munday, an opponent of the City Council schemes, who had, with Right Hon. Isaac Foot, PC, organised an international petition to seek the help of the Commission. Mr Samuel said that he would prepare a report for the Commissioners *'who would then decide what action would be taken.'*

Two weeks later a letter arrived from Queen Anne's Gate, SW1, from the Royal Fine Art Commission in which the Commission confirmed: *'its opinion that the Barbican is an area of exceptional architectural and historic interest, and that special measures are required to ensure the preservation of its existing character in any redevelopment.'*

It went on to say, with more than a hint of irony with respect to actions rather than the words: *'The Commission notes that a similar view has been expressed by the City Council, both in the statement attached to the Development Plan and in subsequent declarations.'*

'The Commission is not satisfied, however, that the intention is capable of being carried out successfully under the procedure at present being adopted, and would recommend the removal of this problem from the normal routine procedure under the Town Planning Act and the appointment of a special committee, possibly a joint body drawn from the City Council and from unofficial sources specially interested in the future of the area, to handle all problems concerned with its redevelopment.'

'In this connection, the Commission understands that if an overall plan for the whole area can be prepared and agreed by all those interested, some financial contribution might be available from outside sources as a contribution to those aspects of the redevelopment scheme that would not normally be accepted by the local authority.'

The prospect of funding from outside sources implied the possibility of new doors being opened, and greatly encouraged some members of the City Council. HM Pattinson, a former Conservative Chairman of the Reconstruction Committee, spoke in favour of promoting preservation. Meanwhile, Alderman HM 'Bert' Medland, Labour, complained that the Council were being *'urged to pander to the whims and fancies of "old women" who, without running the dangers of an election, wanted to do the Council's job. There were,'* he said, *'far too many such people in Plymouth.'*

'The job was the Council's responsibility, and so far,' he claimed, *'they hadn't done too badly. The Barbican,'* he said, *'is a slum area. It should be treated as such.'*

Eighteen months on the arguments were still unresolved. The Housing Committee was accused of trying to obtain every penny it could, reasonable enough in a normal situation, but as had been contended many times, by many organisations, the Barbican was not a normal location. However, *'pressed by the still-long waiting lists and the shortage of land,'* the Committee *'saw squalor rather than history.'*

The new flats at Woolster Street were being built and tragically the Old Ring of Bells, Plymouth's oldest inn, had been demolished to permit street-widening and further housing development. Together with the fact that further compulsory purchase orders for other parts of the Barbican area had recently been confirmed, it was time, according to an un-named *Western Morning News* journalist, *'to re-examine the city's proposals for its historic quarter.'*

The writer was Crispin Gill, Charles Bracken's erstwhile pupil, who had been with the *Western Morning News* since 1934 and who had been made assistant editor in 1950. Mr Gill was also married to Isaac Foot's niece, Molly.

The article, which appeared on 24 January 1957 ran: *'The Barbican has been a battlefield ever since the Plan for Plymouth was drawn up. Those anxious to preserve it have constantly fought a rearguard action against those who simply pronounce it unfit to live in and are anxious to sweep it away.'*

The article was partly an update, partly a restatement of the whys and wherefores of *'The dangers of treating old Plymouth as a slum clearance area'*. In it Gill, who was firmly on the side of the preservationists, was keen to point out that the 'preservers' were by no means looking to keep everything, especially not the *'cottages built in the gardens of earlier houses, filling up the empty fields between the town and the Hoe, creating dark, miserable back-to-back tenements … They agree that much rebuilding is necessary.'*

But, argued the writer, *'this is an area for reconstruction, not for a plain housing project.'*

The late-lamented Ring of Bells, Woolster Street, photographed from various angles.

The ancient entrance to the Ring of Bells.

'At any time now on a summer's day the coaches can be counted around this area in their scores. They bring money to Plymouth, but visitors will not come to see blocks of flats that might be in Poplar or Liverpool.'

'To "municipalize" this corner of Plymouth would be fatal. With few houses incorporating the materials of the old, with the character still about the courts and stairs, with the open spaces used for boats rather than flower beds, this could still be a showpiece.'

Part of the spark for igniting the cooling embers of this oft heated debate had undoubtedly been the demolition of the Old Ring of Bells. This was the building that Southcombe Parker had said in 1943 'should definitely be retained and the street widening be done of the opposite side'; this was the building that as recently as 1951 had appeared in the official guide to 'Listed Buildings' in the area as a Grade II monument:

'1580-1600. The structure may be older. C.18 plaster front of 3 storeys, 4 windows. 4-centred granite doorway with carved spandrels. Interior has C.16 door-frames, panelling, and enriched plaster ceiling with frieze. At rear is small oak window with trefoil head. Remains of skittle alley to north of yard.'

In other words this was not only Plymouth's oldest surviving inn, it was full of period pieces that could have made it one of the area's greatest attractions. But it was in a parlous state and, more importantly, it was in the way of the Corporation's plans. Plans which, in January 1957, now spoke of: '... razing all the houses from Lambhay-hill right across Castle-street and New-street to the back of the Southside-street houses, demolishing enough slum properties and putting up enough blocks of flats to win the subsidies. The area would be treated simply as a housing project, a slum-clearance area, with 32, New-street – given to the city by the Old Plymouth Society – standing alone and forlorn among the new and overpowering blocks.'

The situation was different now, to what it had been just two years earlier: '... the Government has taken subsidies away. It has put emphasis on slum-clearance. If a certain number of slum dwellings are razed and blocks of flats of at least four storeys in height are built, then subsidies can still be obtained.'

'Many houses need replacing,' conceded Gill, adding, 'it needs light and air. Yet the ground plan of interlocked courtyards and winding alleys and a few of the houses all cry aloud for retention.'

Under the proposals of 1955, when the debate had last been really heated, 'the first plan for the corner from Lambhay-hill to Castle-street' had been to largely keep the existing street plan and by building flats 'in the vernacular' to 'retain the character of the fishing village'. A character 'that could match the show pieces of the Cornish coast'.

However, this no longer looked likely and Gill was doing his best to fan the flames once more: 'There is little enough left of Plymouth as it was. Surely a proud city can save something of its history.'

'Whitehall's slum-clearance plans and the subsidies designed to speed those plans, were never intended to destroy such a corner as this. Would it not listen to a plea for consideration, waive some of the calls for all four-storey flats, make some concession for new building which would preserve atmosphere and character?'

Thanks to the earlier protests, the Woolster Street flats had at least received an extra allowance, permitting slate-hung frontages. More recently: '... when the Barbican itself was resurfaced, the old cobbles were lifted, the road levelled, and the cobbles relaid. It probably cost more than throwing away the cobbles and sending along the machine that lays a carpet of tar, but it was worthwhile, and it still is the Barbican.'

'If a mere road surface merits the care, so does the whole area.'

Unwittingly perhaps, Gill's last comment raised a new issue – what was 'the whole area'?

That week a minute of the Housing Committee proposed that:

'The redevelopment area should proceed on the basis that only the character of the Barbican area proper – for example New-street, Pin-lane, Castle-street, and Lambhay-hill – should be retained.'

Mr Leslie F Paul, for the Conservatives, pointed out that in the Plan For Plymouth 'old Plymouth was spread over a much wider area and included one side of Ebrington-street, St Andrew-street, and Notte-street. It was not right,' he added, 'for a single committee to repudiate the plan.'

Castle Street, the south side, demolished to make way for housing.

No.s 1-3 Vauxhall Street. Demolished to make way for flats.

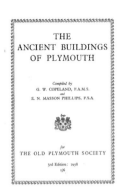

THE
ANCIENT BUILDINGS
OF PLYMOUTH

Compiled by
G. W. COPELAND, F.A.M.S.
and
E. N. MASSON PHILLIPS, F.S.A.

for
THE OLD PLYMOUTH SOCIETY
3rd Edition: 1958
1/6

Stanley, who was to be for many years the Secretary of the Old Plymouth Society, certainly knew better than most, but his point was that not only had the Council requested various reports into this very issue several times over the previous fifteen years, they should also have been aware of the 1955 update of the *Ancient Buildings of Plymouth* which Masson Phillips and Copeland had recently compiled for the Old Plymouth Society and which was available for 1/6d.

Remarkably, the casualties among the lists of worthy buildings in the ten years since the War, were comparatively slight compared to the ten years before the War. No.s 1 to 6 Vauxhall Street had all gone, despite the fact that two of them survived the war intact and only one had been totally destroyed. No.s 1 to 3 Exeter Street, a group of three seventeenth-century properties, had gone - as had the Household of Faith building, Hampton House in Ebrington Street and four properties in Hoe Street. But there were menacing developments on the horizon:

'According to the Medical Officer of Health, 56 houses "in New Street or nearby" are "unfit for human habitation" or are, by reason of their bad arrangement, or the narrowness or bad arrangement of the streets, dangerous or injurious to the health of the inhabitants (Western Independent 3 February 1957).'

Mr Hugh Dent, a member of the committee of the Old Plymouth Society, said they were very concerned about the proposals and reminded the City Engineer's Department that they had promised to consult them before destroying any building of value: *'We battled for the Old Ring O'Bells and lost, and the Ministry of Works were very angry about it – we have the support of the Ministry in our efforts to preserve local buildings of architectural and historic interest.'*

Clearly, however, it wasn't enough.

Opening what was to be a two-hour Council debate on the topic on 5 February, Robert Briscoe (Labour) complained of the delay caused by consultation with the Minister: *'I'm getting a little tired of the dilly-dallying and with those people who became "gooey-eyed" about buildings of architectural interest.'*

Speaking as a Labour councillor – although the issue split both parties – William Oats said: *'it is time to stop this nonsense of preserving something because it was built in the Elizabethan era.'*

Clearly not everyone on the Council derived any pleasure from considering the distant past, but some it seems not only struggled with the distant past, they struggled with the recent past. In a letter to the *Western Morning News* a few days later Stanley Goodman (a solicitor, councillor and another Foot relative) wrote: *'It is reported that the Housing Committee of Plymouth City Council have asked the Chief Sanitary Inspector for a report on "unfit" buildings which ought to be preserved for their historic or architectural importance (if any).'*

'What do they mean by the words 'if any'? Don't they know the identity of these buildings?'

Notte Street, 1951, work has begun on the new NAAFI club, meanwhile the buildings opposite and just a little further down on both sides are all destined for demolition.

Meanwhile Stanley Goodman, another Labour councillor, said: *'Some of us are of the opinion that if you allow sporadic demolition in New-street and Southside-street, you will destroy once and for all the whole value of that particular historic precinct.'*

The latest proposal he suggested was diametrically opposed to previously-declared Council policy. The authors of the 1943 Plan had written:

'We consider that it is most desirable to rehabilitate the present buildings and so re-create character without disturbing existing layout.'

'The tragedy of this debate,' he added, *'is that one of the authors of that Plan is about 14 feet in front of me, but has to remain silent.'* [Goodman was referring to Paton Watson]

Mr Goodman also made reference to Mr Bienawski's Plan for the Barbican, to which Bill Miller later replied: *'No such plan has ever been seen in the architect's office and no such plan is known. A report was submitted by an employee, but we have no plan. If a plan exists, it exists purely on a private basis, sponsored by whom I neither know nor care. It was not sponsored by the Corporation.'*

Perhaps not, but having been produced by a member of the City Architect's office it had all the hall marks of a thoroughly well-researched report and had obviously involved long hours of interviewing and ground work. There was also the matter of the *1951 Schedule of Listed Buildings*, the 1948 report from the Society for the Protection of Ancient Buildings, the more recent report from the Fine Art Commission and the informed and by no means fanciful suggestions from the Old Plymouth Society, the Plymouth Institution and the Port of Plymouth Chamber of Commerce. There could be little doubt that certain members of the Council were being incredibly cavalier in their attitude to the heritage of the City and to the opinions of those whose opinions were normally valued.

The bottom line, inevitably, was a financial one: *'Preservation costs money and would mean the loss of a subsidy,'* warned Miller, while Bert Medland added: *'it all boils down to how much money you are prepared to pay for the preservation of a lot of rubbish down on the Barbican.'*

Small wonder that one councillor proposed that the City's coat of arms be amended to: *'... two bulldozers rampant on a sea of rubble.'*

The *Western Morning News* leader column that day was unequivocal: *'In the South Kensington Museum can be seen one of the first aeroplanes, made of bamboo and canvas. Nobody suggest that because it is unsafe to fly that is a reason for burning it. Nobody argues that the old Rocket, prototype of locomotives, should be broken up because it is unfit for modern traffic. When then, should that be the only argument for buildings? What is required for the Barbican, as for all such historic areas, is the production of an overall plan, by which the Council will know at each stage where it is going.'*

Meanwhile GW Copeland, one of the authors of the most recent schedule of Ancient Buildings wrote to the *Morning News* to remind those who would sanction the bulldozers that all of the aforementioned and readily dismissed 'reports' including the 1943 Plan, had all recommended preserving that which was deemed to be worthwhile and that across all these documents there was little disagreement about what 'worthwhile' meant.

Part of the problem was that the Corporation already owned many of these so-called slums and were keen to get a move on, but writing in the *Morning News*, the day after the debate, Stanley Goodman wrote:

'The Romans used to define ownership as being the right to 'use, abuse, or destroy' the thing owned. If we now abuse or destroy this heritage, for want of a little money, our successors will want to erect another plaque in New Street. This plaque will say:

'To the everlasting infamy of the Housing Committee of Plymouth City Council which in the year 1957 sold five hundred years of history for a mess of subsidies.'

Neither was this debate confined to the older 'gooey-eyed' members of the community, as a meeting that week of the Junior Chamber of Commerce, bore witness. Charles Harding said that if no plan for the area existed then one should be produced, but felt that if the Chamber were to produce one it would *'receive no consideration'* and Stanley Edgcumbe noted that other cities seemed to take a pride in their old building but not so Plymouth Corporation. Notwithstanding all of that it was decided that the Reconstruction Committee of the Chamber should look into the Barbican question.

Stirling, Samuels, Mason and Jellicoe study a model of the proposed new City Centre. Rightt; Jellicoe, Samuels, Stedman and Stirling pay a visit to the Barbican.

Two days later, as fate would have it, Godfrey Samuel, the Secretary of the Royal Fine Art Commission was back in Plymouth to look at the proposals for Plymouth's civic precinct, with him this time was the fifty-seven year-old architect Geoffrey Jellicoe. Jellicoe had worked on a number of post-war town plans (Wolverhampton, Guildford, Wellington, Sutton-on-Sea) and was already well on the way to being recognised as the most significant landscape architect of his generation. His visit to Plymouth was extended to take stock of the *'sleeping issue of the Barbican which had raged into fresh controversy'* (WMN).

The two visitors had received 'representations' from two Plymouth people acting independently of the City Council: Mr HW Woollcombe, the Plymouth solicitor who represented the Port of Plymouth Chamber of Commerce at the local inquiry back in 1955, and the Vice-Chairman of the Junior Chamber, Peter Stedman.

Together with Alderman Harry Mason (the post-war Labour leader and then Chairman of the Reconstruction Committee who lived in Isaac Foot's old house in Lipson Terrace), Lloyd Jones, the Town Clerk, and City Architect, Stirling, the party set off on a tour of the New Street area and the houses there now threatened with demolition.

'The Royal Fine Art Commission is a body which advises the Ministry of Housing and Local Government on developments of major importance," explained the *Morning News*, adding, *'it is the Minister of Housing who will decide whether any of the properties in the proposal 'have any special architectural or historic merit' warranting their preservation.'*

The press pressure via the *Western Morning News* was maintained throughout that month; Hilary Cornish wrote from Crownhill advising those few councillors who did not know what a valuable asset the Barbican is to:

'look in a Plymouth guide book (or any other town guide) and the emphasis is on the old parts, these are the places everyone wants to see first.' A sentiment echoed by Alan Black of Hartley: 'Remember that Looe, Polperro, St Ives, and many other places make the greater part of their living from similar "slums".'

On Sunday 10 February the editor of the *Western Independent* joined in, the lengthy leader ending thus: 'The Barbican area is not just a site for another Swilly or an Efford, but an integral part of our enriched old Plymouth. It is no place for the demolition gangs and the stucco experts.'

The following day, Monday, the Lord Mayor, William Oats, repeated his views on the Barbican 'hovels' while addressing the Dicken's Fellowship at Dingle's Dartmoor Restaurant. While on the Tuesday, Humphrey Woollcombe told the Chamber of Commerce that following the meeting with the Fine Arts Commissioners a way forward for the Barbican was now possible.

On the Thursday the *Morning News* repeated Sir Phillip Pilditch's newspaper article from 1929 – 'the issues of 30 years ago are being fought out again. The words of 30 years ago are applicable now as they were then.'

Back then the scheme that had occasioned the creation of the Old Plymouth Society was the: '... obliteration of the lines of the old streets known as New-street and Castle-street and, among the courts, of Cambers and Cooksley's.' And now precisely those same areas were facing the axe again. The only difference was that when Sir Phillip's piece was first published Plymouth still had about sixty houses featuring the local Tudor/ Jacobean 'specialty':– 'the circular staircase around a ship's mast newel' – a feature that Southcombe Parker maintained was 'peculiar to Plymouth', while now there were 'probably less than twenty' and several of those were in New Street.

Over the next week or so the *Herald* and the *Morning News* continued to drip feed pro-preservation pieces into their pages and then on 19 February the story hit the national news as *The Times* featured an article 'History Conflicts With Planning' from their 'special correspondent'. A brief resumé of the saga followed and the story ended with perhaps the most sensible suggestion yet:

'Some device is needed,' suggested Alderman HG Mason, leader of the city council: 'to allow the local authority to rehouse the occupants under the terms of the Housing Subsidies Act, 1956, without observing the requirement that the vacated property should be demolished. The buildings might then be retained for preservation, but I consider that the cost of restoration would be so great that it is altogether unlikely that the council could undertake any such scheme unaided.'

Speaking that same day on the Barbican, addressing a meeting of Sutton Women Conservatives, Harold Pattinson, the vice-chairman of Plymouth Housing Committee, said: 'People who were interested in preserving ancient and historic buildings on the Barbican should start a fund and buy them from the Corporation at their site value. Provided that no-one lives in them they would not need to be pulled down. They could be converted into antique shops or old-world tea shops. They would revive the Barbican and it would become a world-wide attraction.'

Later that week there was news that the Housing Committee were seeking a loan of over £40,000 to acquire land in High Street, The Parade, Vauxhall Street and Palace Street under six compulsory purchase orders 'recently confirmed by the Minister'. 'Rehousing people displaced and demolition would follow the acquisition of the land.'

The timing of the announcement seemed odd. Nevertheless, the following day, the *Western Morning News* published a letter from a collection of 'Plymothians of some long standing and having no close connections with the City Council' who wanted to make an 'appeal for the consideration of the future of the Barbican area in a way which future generations of Plymothians will approve'. The signatories included Stanley Edgcumbe, Hilary Cornish, Southcombe Parker, Humphrey Woollcombe, John Foot and Randolph Churchill.

The following day the same paper published a missive from five Barbican residents who 'wish to state that we are anxious to remain resident in the area, and, at the same time, wish the historic atmosphere of the area to be maintained.' The signatories to this epistle were Cullen and Briggs from Lambhay Hill, Vincent from Lambhay Street, Higgins from Castle Street and Wills from Stoke's Lane.

At this point an unlikely voice entered the debate. Sir Patrick Abercrombie, giving his address as Brooks's Club, St James Street, SW1, wrote to The

Times. Identifying himself as *'joint author of 'A Plan For Plymouth'* Sir Patrick dismissed remarks about *'uninhabitable showpieces'* and *'subsidies by demolition'* and he too quoted Sir Phillip Pilditch, much as the *Morning News* had earlier that month:

'I would also add that the narrow streets and the intimate urban atmosphere are exactly what we miss in our new towns and slick housing schemes. From my former study of the Barbican and house to house visits, I am convinced that it can be satisfactorily reconditioned, hygienically and architecturally. But I entirely agree with my old friend Alderman Mason that special aid and treatment are required.'

Before the short month was out *'the controversy went one stage further, when the area was featured in a BBC television programme'.* 'Millions' according to the *Western Independent* watched Stanley Goodman, appearing as a member of the Old Plymouth Society rather than as a councillor, along with Dr Pierson, the Medical Officer and Lloyd Jones the Town Clerk. A number of residents were asked how they felt about leaving the Barbican and they *'all appeared to want to remain where they were and thought that the houses should be left alone.'*

On Thursday 28 February the Housing Committee announced that it was prepared to let any Corporation owned buildings on a 99-year lease, for non-residential use, provided that offers are made for them within three months of the following Monday's Council meeting. That same day Jim Woodrow wrote to the Town Clerk, sending copies to Bert Medland and Sir Clifford Tozer, saying that a special sub-committee of the Old Plymouth Society had been appointed, with him as chairman and with the object of assisting the Council in the historic quarter.

'We are willing to raise a fund again (as the OPS had done thirty years earlier) by public subscription, and indeed substantial offers of financial help have already been made to us, from within the city and afar. But we are not sure that the purchase of a number of houses for non-residential use, which would create dead areas in what should be a district alive and vital, is the solution.'

Mr Woodrow, speaking on behalf of the organisation – the Old Plymouth Society - which had increased its membership from 65 to over 250 in the course of the previous ten days - then requested a month's deferment *'to enter into discussions with us so that best possible use can be made of the private help envisaged'.*

Doomed cottages at the top of Castle Dyke Lane

Above: *The new City Centre takes shape and the doomed buildings on the north side of Whimple Street make ready to face the demolition men.*
Opposite page: *The soon-to-be-removed buildings at the Notte Street junction of Southside Street.*

BITING THE BULLET

The First of March 1957 was a Friday, it was also St David's Day and speaking at the St David's Dinner and Dance of the Cymmrodorion Society of Plymouth at the Duke of Cornwall that evening the Lord Mayor, William Oats, replying to those who advocating the preservation of the Barbican repeated his mantra that the *'hovels will have to come down'*.

Mr W Lloyd Williams, proposing the toast said: *'The future of the Barbican is the $64,000 question which the people of Plymouth were asking. Plymouth'* he said, *'had reached world fame and renown during the reign of Queen Elizabeth, and it was not difficult to understand the desire of many citizens to hold on to the remains of her history. It is to be hoped that a solution to the conflicting views and interests will be found.'*

As it happened a solution was not that far away, and in part it was brought yet closer thanks to a letter published earlier that day in *The Times*, from 'Esher'.

Viscount Esher was the Chairman of the Society for the Protection of Ancient Buildings and it would appear from his letter that he and his committee were unaware just how little attention had been paid to their report of eight years earlier.

'The committee is surprised that no reference (in the previous pieces published in The Times) has been made to the fact that in 1949 the

society was asked by the Plymouth City Council to prepare a report on the Barbican area and that a detailed scheme for dealing with it was worked out by two of the society's experts (both well-known architects) and submitted to the corporation.'*

'If this report is examined, it will be found that the problem was dealt with in no exclusively antiquarian spirit and that a considerable amount of demolition was envisaged. The society is still convinced that if these suggestions were acted upon the cost would not be considered immense. It is also of the opinion that not only would the general outline and atmosphere of the Barbican be preserved, but that a large part of the expense could be met by the increased rateable value of the area which would occur when the buildings were made more attractive to a more remunerative class of tenant.'

'As there is apparently much controversy dividing the city, it should be pointed out that it is not a question of rebuilding the area or of retaining historic dwellings as "unhabitable showpieces". If a few of the 90 copies of the report the society was asked to supply were made open to public inspection, it will be found that the whole point of the scheme is that all the buildings retained could and should be reconditioned and made attractive to tenants. It should not be difficult to bring the sanitary requirements up to the standards of today.'

No.s 1-3 Southside Street, cleared to make way for new flats.

'*The society also wishes to stress the historical importance of the area and the loss both of prestige and income which would occur if the city showed itself so insensible to its past.*'

For the 'keepers' this news was electrifying, for the 'sweepers' it was frustrating and for those who had filed the report away in the first place, it was profoundly embarrassing. The Plan that everyone had been asking for, for so many years, had been in the Council's very hands all this time – 90 copies of it. Where had they all gone, surely if any of the Councillors favouring preservation had known about it they would have shouted about it, was Viscount Esher overstating his case or did the report really offer a viable solution?

The *Western Morning News* lost no time in getting their hands on a copy and the very next day they published the Society's major conclusions alongside the current council proposals. In some instances they matched perfectly.

'*Pin Lane. All existing buildings it is advised, should be cleared in Pin-lane, Havelock-place and Lucknow-place ... This is also the council's plan,*' noted the newspaper.

'*Southside Street. A street of both attractive and ugly buildings which we propose should be retained as a shopping centre*' ran the report, while '*the council proposes demolishing No.s 2, 3 and 4.*'

With Lambhay Hill the report again appeared to be much in accord with the Council's views, but actually there was a subtle change and one that very much mirrors the contemporary approach now, in the twenty-first century: '*No buildings of value in the area bounded by Lambhay-street and Lambhay-hill. The whole site should be cleared and a block of more expensive flats built with terraced gardens, forecourts, etc. overlooking the water.*'

In this last statement the Society were proposing what now seems obvious, but despite sitting on the report for eight years no member of the council had yet proposed that the area might be upgraded in terms of its housing, which considering the views available, was surprising. However there is evidence to suggest that when the new flats were built the Corporation's policy to filling the new accommodation was skewed in favour of the white collar workers as headmasters and lawyers were among the first wave of new council tenants. Private housing wasn't as affordable as it later became and the bombing of residential areas had been comparatively indiscriminate.

Moving down the hill, the Society recommended knocking down the large stone-walled warehouse at the western end, part of which is, more than fifty years on, still ruinous, and widening the road with flats above lock-up shops, replacing it. Otherwise, they recommended reconditioning and preserving sixteen of the historic properties that the Council was now proposing to demolish. There was a similar story in Looe Street where the Society advocated the retention of a dozen or so dwellings that the Council wanted to remove.

All in all this was pretty much the report everyone had been clamouring for and the Council had been sitting on it for eight years. The Chamber and other organisations had repeatedly been requesting that the Council take no action until, with the help of an architect, a Plan had been produced specifically for the Barbican and here was the very thing, compiled by not one, but two eminently qualified architects – John Macgregor, a Fellow of the Society of Antiquaries and of the Royal Institute of British Architects, and David D Nye, an architect member of the Incorporated Association of Architects, and a licentiate of the Royal Institute of British Architects.

Small wonder, therefore, that Viscount Esher should be somewhat horrified that the report had been quietly pigeon-holed and the ninety copies (enough for every member of the council, the local press and others) apparently undistributed.

What message were the Council trying to send to this august body by ignoring their recommendations and their offer of help?

'The Society would welcome the opportunity of training further students by collaborating with the City Council in the preparation of surveys and plans and the supervision of the work proposed in the report. If the City Council would consider such an arrangement, the Society feels that its principles and methods of repair could be demonstrated with advantage to the people of Plymouth and to all others concerned in the preservation of ancient buildings which form so important a part of the national heritage.'

The heat was on. Harold Pattinson, as Vice-Chairman of the Housing Committee, now wrote to *The Times* putting the Council's view:

'New Street, could be saved, if the desire is strong enough, but the houses would have to be privately owned and not let as houses. Failure to destroy or make the arrangements suggested means forfeiting a subsidy for New Street alone worth £1,000 a year for 60 years. Castle Street and Lambhay Hill are already subject of compulsory purchase orders confirmed after very little opposition, and nothing can be done now. It is still possible to keep what is really attractive and historic – Barbican, the Mayflower stone and steps, Southside Street, and Sutton Pool. If this be achieved, most will be content, but there remains the question – who pays?'

As that day's copy of The Times was being read the length and breadth of the Country, the Plymouth City Council chamber flatly refused to extend from three months to six the period in which private individuals or organisations interested in preserving condemned houses on the Barbican could apply to lease them for non-residential use.

The Chairman of the Housing Committee, Bill Miller, said that Council had spent £38,000 in 1929 on acquiring and adapting the houses in New Street and Castle Street, and another £24,000 since in keeping them in repair. The bill would not be finally paid until 1992. He added *'had it not been for the delay caused by the Old Plymouth Society rehousing would have been started two and half years ago.'*

Cooksley Court and the steps leading up to Lambhay Street.

'A sketch indicating the effect that would be produced if some of the warehouses were reduced in height to a more harmonious skyline and the harbour adapted to yachting and similar pleasure activities' WMN 5 March 1957.

Alderman Mason agreed: *'The first of a series of reports on the Barbican was drawn up in 1927. As a result, the then Chairman of the Housing Committee, Mr Albert Webb, proposed reconditioning and the extraordinary thing was that some of the houses Sir Clifford Tozer saw on Sunday were reconditioned then. They were considered unfit for human habitation in 1927, now within 30 years, despite reconditioning, they were unfit again. Fundamentally these houses could not stand reconditioning, and people should not continue to live in them.'*

Pattinson added his voice: *'I saw the houses cannot be made fit to live in as accommodation.'*

Sir Clifford Tozer was proposing that the Old Plymouth Society be given six months to come up with a scheme and not just three months, but Robert Briscoe felt that the amendment should be treated with suspicion: *'the resurrected Old Plymouth Society seems to have its ear on the Press, on radio, and television – with the result that the public get a biased view.*

Cut the cackle and get on with the job,' he added, *'because there is no chance of the Old Plymouth Society being able to take advantage of the amendment.'*

In a long and lively debate Councillor Miller suggested that *'there was no sincerity in the letter from the Old Plymouth Society'*, while countering Stanley Goodman argued that the Medical Officer of Health was *'condemning certain properties, not because they were unfit but because the streets were too narrow.'*

At the end of it all the Council approved the recommendation that *'the Royal Fine Art Commission be supplied with the suggested layout of the Woolster-street, Lambhay-street, and Castle-street areas, together with a map showing the premises affected by clearance orders and the Medical Officer's representations.'*

Dr Pierson, had reported to the Committee that in his opinion the only satisfactory way of dealing with the conditions in the area was the demolition of all the buildings, but at his suggestion it was proposed that the Minister be asked if any of the properties have special architectural or historic merit which would warrant their preservation.

And so it was revealed that after surveys conducted by various expert bodies and individuals in 1918, 1929, 1938, 1942, 1949, 1951 and 1955, all of which were in close agreement, there were still members of the City Council who did not know which properties 'if any' had any special architectural merit. Perhaps the media presentation had been a little one-sided, but with such a level of ignorance existing within the Council, despite a number of those very reports having been commissioned by the Council, who could blame them.

The following day, 5 March, Charles Harding, presenting the report of the Junior Chamber's Reconstruction Committee, found it difficult to understand why, *'after spending public money on the report prepared by the Society for the Preservation of Ancient Buildings, it was not made available to the public.'*

Peter Stedman agreed and added, *'there is an unfortunate impression that those who wished to preserve the Barbican, wish to keep it as it is, this is not true, no-one is disputing that people should be rehoused.'* As for their being *'no chance'* that the Old Plymouth Society would be able to take advantage of the situation, the day after the Council debate the Junior

Chamber agreed to endorse the action of the Society; Stanley Edgcumbe argued that this was now the only way of saving the Barbican – *'if we wish to be helpful, members should back up the efforts of the society in every way.'*

The Old Plymouth Society themselves having noted shelving of the 1943 Plan and the ignoring of the 1949 SPAB's report, decided to engage *'an architect of repute, experience in old buildings'* to advise them on the leasing of the threatened old buildings. While not understanding the *'need for present haste'* (ie the Council wanting an answer within three months), particularly when *'nothing has been done on the Barbican for so long'*, the Society, or individuals working in association with the Society, they said, would take the leaseholds of certain of these houses. At a meeting of its executive at the Prysten House on Friday 8 March they resolved that *'a fund will be launched on a scale to enable this to be done.'*

In a carefully-worded statement they added: *'It might well be that if an overall survey were made and a plan prepared, in which careful restoration and preservation went hand in hand with development, the financial burden falling on the city would in the end be less than would be involved in the Council's present proposals.'*

Despite the cynicism of certain members of the City Council, there appeared to be general support for the preservationists: *'If Mr Miller thinks opinions like those personified by the Old Plymouth Society are those of people of audacity and cheek, he is likely to find many such, both in and out of Plymouth,'* wrote Tex Rundle in a letter to the *Herald's* postbag, while the delegates of the Plymouth Standing Conference of Women's Organisations also spoke out in support of the sentiments of the OPS *'and felt that much of the Barbican might be retained.'*

Meanwhile, another lady, Mrs MM Cload, Life-President of the Sutton Harbour Regatta Committee, spoke out at her committee's annual meeting the following week, held in the Seaman's Bethel at the bottom of Castle Street:

'Saying she felt bitter about the many adverse comments made about the Barbican recently, Mrs Cload denied that the people responsible for neglecting the property were the residents – "the blame is on the landlords and the city of Plymouth themselves." She added that people living on the Barbican realised that some of the houses were very old but failure to look after houses over a period of twenty years after they had been redecorated was not a fault that could be attached to the residents (WMN 18 March).

Looe Street and New Street, mid-1957.

Rear of 34 New Street.

Others too spoke out. John Foot, addressing the annual meeting of Devon and Cornwall Liberal Federation on Saturday 16 March, said the City Fathers were *'pulling down the Barbican merely to lay their hands on a few miserable subsidies.'* William Roseveare, an eminent Plymouth architect, felt that the Barbican should be *'retained as an historic showplace. Professional advice,'* he said, *'would help remedy 'eyesores' in the area and blitzed sites could be developed for housing in keeping with the character.'*

The *Herald* conducted a six-question survey on the debate:

1. Are you interested in the future of the Barbican area which has been the subject of recent controversy? To which 95% said yes.
2. Do you consider the Barbican area a financial asset to Plymouth? 81% said yes.
3. Do you consider the Barbican and its associations of cultural value to Plymouth? 84% said yes.
4. Do you favour demolition of all Barbican-area properties which are declared 'unfit' by the Medical Officer of Health, whether or not they are of special historic or architectural interest? To which 75% said no.
5. Do you favour unconditionally the retention of such buildings in any clearance scheme envisaged for the area? To which 56% agreed.
6. Do you approve of these buildings being preserved provided it does not incur a charge upon the rates? 85% said yes.

5% apparently abstained or didn't answer questions 2 - 6, while several felt that even if it did incur a charge on the rates it would be worth it:

'I think if you are going to preserve something, and it is worth preserving, it should be done. If my rates can pay for the Lord Mayor's Rolls-Royce then they can pay for the preservation of the Barbican,' said Vicar of St Matthias Church, Rev JG Byrnell. While Mrs WE Garland, a barmaid from Efford, said: *'I would like to see the Barbican preserved at all cost. There is nowhere in Plymouth with quite the same amount of colour and atmosphere.'*

Among the residents the feelings were even stronger: *'I was born here, and my children were brought up here. I would like to see the old houses modernised, and the people allowed to live in them,'* said Mrs G Kirton of 12 The Barbican. Many former residents who had left the area *'were clamouring to come back'* she said. Meanwhile, in New Street itself, Mrs E Smith of No.39, said; *'If they take me away from here it will put me in my grave',* and Mrs L Chapman of No.34 added, *'It would break my heart to leave.'*

Notwithstanding these findings, Bill Miller, the Housing Chairman, still claimed, just a few days later, that only 3 or 4% of the inhabitants of the Barbican actually wanted to stay there. Speaking at a 'brains trust' held by the Plymouth branch of the Business and Professional Women's Club at the Duke of Cornwall Hotel, he further said, of New Street specifically, that it was *'absolutely impossible'* for humans to live in some of the properties.

'The electric light is on nearly all the time in every room for people to see. I have had to have temporary lights fitted in the court yards. It is not right that humans beings should live in such conditions, even if they desire to live there.'

Another member of the panel, Miss S Peatfield, headmistress of Stoke Damerel High School for Girls, said she thought the Barbican was something which we: *'should try to keep. It would enrich the life of the city because there was something old and new there.'* Miss Peatfield understood that there were people who were happy to be there now – they ought to be educated out of it. *'The area,'* she said, *'could be used for artist's studios and similar places – it would add to the pleasure of Plymouth.'*

The media attention had never been higher and before the month was out it was announced the Old Plymouth Society had found their architect to advise on *'which properties ought to be preserved and to suggest the nature and extent of the work that might be undertaken,'* said Jim Woodrow in the statement accompanying the announcement – which incidentally was quoted in the *Western Morning News, Evening Herald* and *The Times:*

'There was no doubt,' he said, 'that some of the properties would have to be demolished, but with sympathetic treatment the atmosphere and character of the only remaining part of old Plymouth could be maintained.'

And the architect appointed for the task? John E Macgregor, the same man who, eight years earlier had co-authored the report for the City Council, which that same City Council had chosen to ignore. Perhaps now, with the media spotlight closely following every step of this saga, a little more notice might be taken.

Throughout April 1957 the debate continued. Details were published in the *Morning News* of an eighteenth- century house in White Lane, between New Street and Southside Street, which had recently been restored under the guidance of Ivan Hodges, a local architect, and with the full support and approval of the Housing Committee.

The local Liberals, anxious that the controversy didn't become a political wrangle, urged interested citizens to support the Old Plymouth Society, 'The Bish' and 'Shangri-La' wrote psuedonymously to the *Herald*; the former saying *'Plymouth is now in the 20th century, not the 18th, so let's keep up with the times'* and the latter suggesting that it should be *'the landlords themselves paying for the renovation of the old properties'* (the Council?? – they owned 36 of the 56 threatened properties).

On Saturday, 6 April, the *Western Morning News* published excerpts from another letter, this time not directly sent to the paper but to Hugh Dent, a teacher at Plymouth College. Dent had been an acquaintance of Sir Patrick Abercrombie, the joint-architect of the1943 Plan who had died on 23 March. Just before he died, Sir Patrick had written to his old friend;

'I am sorry about Plymouth. The worst of leaving one's family is that it doesn't often grow up as one meant! Lady Astor is the best stickler for the principles of the Plan … she has always been a fighter for the Barbican – not for the uninhabitable, historic houses, but for pleasant, cosy, and sanitary surroundings in contrast to gaunt but sanitary flats.'

'I don't believe I can do anything – unless you think a letter to the Plymouth papers would have any weight.'

In the event he never produced that letter: 'but,' wrote the *Morning News* journalist [presumably Crispin Gill], *'it is reasonable to believe that he would have liked his opinion on the Barbican to have found public expression.'*

Either way, having mentioned Lady Astor, it was revealed that same day that she was on her way to Plymouth. Having been away in America and then having spent two weeks in Cliveden, she was coming to the city to attend an Old Plymouth Society meeting at the Prysten House.

The Earl of Mount Edgcumbe chaired the meeting and an executive committee was formed, with GA Blakey as treasurer, to raise funds for their intended work. Lady Nancy Astor promised to support the fund. In the meantime the Society's architect, Macgregor, spent a week 'examining the Barbican', which was also visited by WG Hoskins *'whose recent history of Devon is now the accepted authority'* and an Oxford colleague of his, Professor Pantin. *'They spent a day exploring old houses, measuring up a number of them, and making sketch plans. They expressed concern at the idea that any of these old buildings should be demolished,'* said the report on their visit.

On Saturday 13 April the Old Plymouth Society held a talk and a tour of the Barbican. Ted Masson Phillips spoke to the 200-strong audience that packed the little theatre at the bottom of Castle Street and then led as many as wanted to go on a two-hour walk between Lambhay Hill and Looe Street. *'Many residents far from resenting the intrusion, welcomed the visitors and invited them into their homes.'*

White Lane:
Above: *before conversion.*
Below: *after.*

Lady Astor, Peter Stedman, Ted Masson-Phillips, the Earl of Mount Edgcumbe and members of the Old Plymouth Society on a Barbican walkabout.

Gordon Cullen, founder of the Townscape Movement, was sent to Plymouth by the proprietors of the Architectural Review, to give his considered view on the situation.

Cullen's visit had come as direct result of the Junior Chamber of Commerce's 'call for help' sent to the Architectural Review in December, before the Old Plymouth Society had enlisted Macgregor's services. One of the great advantages of bringing an outsider to look at Plymouth's problems is that they inevitably saw the situation from a completely different perspective and before he even began to comment on the Barbican area he permitted himself a slight digression and talked about Plymouth's new shopping centre, which he not only found *'really disappointing from the point of view of planning and architecture'* but *'what is of equal importance is that it is a multiple store centre.'*

His argument now seems quite obvious, but many local authorities failed to appreciate its implications then – and many still fail today.

'When a local shop makes good it prefers to invest its profits rather than pay Income Tax. The investment takes the form of buying out competitors thus forming a local chain of stores. But a multiple store operates differently to a locally established shop: its headquarters may be in London or Manchester and all the services that it needs are provided by salaried employees in London or Manchester. Thus we get the situation whereby the local lawyer and solicitor, the local accountant, the local builder, the local printer and the local signwriter, find themselves out of a job. Gradually the local centre is abandoned by many professional people and many craftsmen and when these valuable stalwarts have gone the area becomes a wasteland; it is on the way to becoming a depressed area, a Dagenham. And since much of the new Plymouth seems to consist of multiple stores, one can draw one's own conclusions. As the chain stores come in so the cream of the local society must emigrate and the vitality of the town is correspondingly reduced.'

'Against this background of sterility we must view the problem of the Barbican for although it is now only a quarter mile square, it is, or could be, a rallying point for all those who want to arrest the devitalisation of provincial England.'

Cullen then proceeded to describe the Barbican area, its industries and its people (*'the population have something of a reputation in Plymouth. Not exactly a dangerous quarter but a bit independent and full-blooded'*). His

'We do so much want to stay here and want to help if we can' one resident said to the apparently lucky reporter who found one of the 3 - 4% of residents who, the Housing Chairman maintained, didn't want to leave the area.

As the Old Plymouth Society's architect was busy working up his report, another highly respected professional in the field, the forty-three-year-old visual impressions were interesting: *'The atmosphere, is reminiscent of St Malo or some small French town and I kept catching the echo of a whiff of Gauloise cigarettes. There is an unbroken thread of architectural style from Elizabethan to modern including Renaissance, Georgian, Victorian industrial and Art Noveau all interwoven ...'*

'It is unique 'not only is it a continuous growth of architectural style, not only is the planning both intimate and exciting, not only is it an area of mixed and complementary uses, but it is lived in by people who are firmly attached to it. This has to be seen as one thing, a sort of style-plan-use population constriction. It is my view that unless we can present the Barbican in this way, unless we can make it dramatically clear and obvious to all that by some miracle Plymouth possesses this unique asset, then we shall not succeed.'

The architect then outlined the *'... problem - slum clearance and the well being of human beings coming before the value of historic precincts'* debate and concluded that the *'actual solution of the problem of what to do to make the area sanitary, etc. is comparatively simple.'* But *'there are four forms of blindness we shall have to cure;*

1 Blindness caused by antiquarianism. The twentieth century respects the sixteenth century but knocks down the nineteenth. Even the eighteenth.

2 Blindness caused by an unwavering faith in bye-laws concerning angles of light, etc. Science is given to us to try and make things work, not to destroy them if they offend. To knock down the Barbican because it offends the bye-laws is like shooting all people with stomach ulcers.

3 Blindness caused by aesthetic orthodoxy. Why is the Commercial Inn to be pulled down? Because they wish to build flats behind it and the Commercial would block the view out to the harbour. So it is to be demolished. This is an intriguing argument. On this basis the flats themselves are due to be knocked down as soon as built in order to let the people behind them have a view of the sea. Where does it all end? If you want a view of the sea the best place to go is to the edge of the sea or exploit a change of level.

4 Blindness caused by convention. Looking at the plan we see a typical hugger-mugger of streets with here and there a public building and an inn. We tend to regard it as just a bit more of that obsolete, outdated city pattern which makes us yawn and turn Progress to Modernisation.'

Lambhay Hill and Castle Street in 1957, from Cullen's article.'

Part of Cullen's solution was to build *'flats stacked at different heights, some two storey, some six, and, I propose, some ten.'* But the key was variation in harmony with the existing variety;

'Compare the arid mono-scenery of a block of flats or a housing estate with the rich variety ... in fifty yards you move from one place to another, from one society to another. Within the overall unity, style, colour and character, modulate and change. The essential pattern exists; all it needs is bringing up to date.'

'We are up against one difficulty, and that is that the operation of conversion will be more expensive and require more application of the brain than knocking down and rebuilding. We must also take the greatest care to avoid the impression that we are solely interested in the quaint and are simply putting the whole thing into deep freeze. The lay public will understand our point of view and even see a lot of sense in it because it will guarantee the tourist industry. In fact what we are doing is tackling the problem of the decaying hearts of towns and trying to keep them alive and personal and urban, not suburban and anonymous.'

'The Barbican case in not in the least concerned with creating an artificial picturesque historical enclave full of arty ne'er-do-wells. It is a living, developing organism of ordinary hard working folk. Far from being obsolete and at the end of its life, it points the way to the town of the future and to destroy it would be another vote cast in favour of the technological wilderness we call Subtopia.'

Camber's Court

The vote-casting analogy was an apposite one as the City Councillors were gearing themselves up for the Local Elections on 2 May and the Barbican was one of the prime issues for candidates of the main parties: *'Although the Conservative and Labour parties each has a definite party line, there are rebels on either side of the fence,'* reported the *Western Independent*. The Conservatives under Sir Clifford Tozer, were, with the exception of one or two members, opposed to wholesale demolition. While the Labour Party's policy *'stresses the need to rehouse people living in slum properties and considers anything else of secondary importance'*, but not every member was prepared to toe that line and Stanley Goodman, who was the Labour Councillor for St Aubyn was, in his own words, working hard

within the Old Plymouth Society, to prevent the Council committing *'a hasty and permanent folly.'*

In the event the election result was to keep the control of the Council in Labour's hands, where it had been since 1953. The 1959 result would be different, but that's jumping too far ahead.

On Saturday, 4 May, it was announced in the *Western Morning News* that Macgregor's first report to the Old Plymouth Society had now been submitted and furthermore that this announcement had been *'deliberately delayed until after the municipal elections so that it would not be brought into politics in any way.'* In other words, further alienating the Labour party by making it a political issue was only likely to back-fire if Labour, as they would be, were to be re-elected. Furthermore, as John Foot (a member of Executive Committee of the OPS and a son of Isaac) was, diplomatically, to put it at a public meeting later that month: *'We all know that in the City Engineer and the City Architect we have men of the very highest qualifications and we want to benefit from their advice. We don't want to fight the Corporation: we want to work in co-operation with it.'*

There was also news of that public meeting to be held at Abbey Hall on Thursday 23 May with *'Mr AL Rowse, the Westcountry historian and Mr John Betjeman, the writer and commentator upon architecture'* ... *'a number of people of similar national repute have already consented to become patrons of the appeal.'*

Betjeman, best remembered these days as a poet, was a respected architectural commentator: he had been an assistant editor on the *Architectural Review* from 1930-35. In 1934 his guide to Cornwall was published as part of the Shell sponsored series from the Architectural Press and his Devon volume followed in 1936. By 1948 he had published more than a dozen books, five of which were poetry collections. News of the 23 May meeting at which Betjeman was due to speak, was published in *The Times*, as well as the local press and it was made clear that everyone who was prepared to attend the fund-raising meeting would be given a copy of the statement issued by the Old Plymouth Society's executive committee, after their digestion of the Macgregor report.

It was also announced that the Fund was already standing at £870 having received a very generous donation of £500 from Lady Astor and a cheque from Dr AL Rowse. Other notables who had pledged support included Viscount Esher (Chairman of the Society for the Protection of Ancient

Buildings), Lord Methuen (Associate of the Royal Academy, Fellow of the Society of Antiquaries and member of the Royal Fine Arts Commission) , Earl Fortescue (Lord Lieutenant of Devon), Sir John Carew Pole (Chairman of Cornwall County Council), Sir Albert Richardson (past president of the Royal Academy), Sir Arthur Bryant (the great historian), Dr WG Hoskins (Devon's leading historian), the Hon V Sackville West (poet and novelist) and Fleet Admiral Chester Nimitz of the US Navy (wartime commander of America's Pacific fleet and honorary chairman of the Drake Navigation Guild of California).

There were two sub-committees of the OPS now operating: the Barbican Appeal Fund, chaired by the Earl of Mount Edgcumbe and backed with an accountant, a bank manager, a company director, a social worker and two solicitors; and the Barbican Committee, made up of an engineer, three solicitors, two chartered surveyors, a dentist, a teacher and a writer.'

On Friday, 17 May, one week before the meeting, the Society released their statement to the local press. In it they announced that they were seeking to acquire just over half (thirty) of the threatened Barbican properties in order to preserve them.

It was clear from the statement that the OPS had accepted from the outset that not everything was going to escape hands of the demolition men: '... we told Mr Macgregor that while we were anxious to keep the narrow streets and cobbled areas, we wanted to let in light and air; and that while we had to have a picture of what would happen over the whole area, the immediate problem was the threatened houses which were of historic and architectural value.'

The statement then attempted to convey the whole picture street by street. With regards to Southside Street and Notte Street there was acceptance of the fact that the junction of the two would need to be redeveloped; for Lambhay Hill, Lambhay Street and Castle Street all largely held by the Corporation under Compulsory Purchase Orders already, they accepted that there was little of architectural value and that the City's suggestions: '... for rebuilding with cottages and blocks of flats, using traditional styles and as far as possible native materials, using the fall of the ground to keep the fishing village atmosphere of narrow lanes and courtyards, opening into one another, are acceptable.'

'Havelock-place and Lucknow-place' were dismissed as 'back filling of no value ... it is felt their removal would be an advantage. The Parade,

Camber's Court

[they noted in what smacked of a heavy compromise] *'is safe, apart from the High-street corner, where a compulsory purchase order may bring in blocks of flats.'*

'Woolster-street to Looe-street. The most valuable houses architecturally are at the top of Looe-treet, between the Minerva Inn and the Arts Centre, and several are included in slum clearance orders. The best are very decayed but ought to be restored. New-street. The Hartley of Old Plymouth, where

Top: *Looe Street (Arts Centre on right).* Bottom: *61 High Street.*

sea captains had their houses built along the pathfield from the Barbican across the back of the Hoe to the mills at Millbay, and Stonehouse village. Elizabethan at the bottom and Queen Anne at the top, is the most valuable street of all.'

Mr Macgregor gave this his most detailed consideration and his proposals need setting out:

'Keep the house beside No.32 (the Elizabethan House) and those opposite, making a nice Tudor Group. Keep the block of houses between the two warehouses on the south side with their pole staircases, overhanging fronts and typical internal arrangements. Take down all the worthless houses behind them, tear up the cemented yards, and make gardens at the back, the sunny south side.

'Rebuild No.15 and the former Robin Hood Inn, opposite, but remove the two houses between them to make gardens for the rebuilt houses, with a six-foot garden wall to keep the street line. Take down the houses of no value in the block between Stokes-lane and Pin-lane (save the corner houses), but keep the street line with low buildings or a wall. Keep the two Queen Anne houses at the top of New-street, taking down the less good houses on either side and at the back to give these two houses gardens again enclosed by a 6ft wall to keep the line of New-street, and Castle Dyke-lane.

'Keep the warehouses at the top and turn Highland-cottages into stores, so that the Hoe entrance to New-street is dramatic and patently the entry into something different. All the warehouses in New-street would remain.'

The OPS were going to the Corporation with an offer to buy thirty properties, funded by a non-profit-making company limited by guarantee which was to be formed to administer these properties.

The publicity generated by this story, and by other means, led to an expectant crowd of more than 500 people attending Abbey Hall the following Friday. Plymouth's new Lord Mayor, Louis F Paul, who unlike his outspoken Labour predecessor was a keen supporter of the Preservationists, described the occasion as *'the most important public meeting in Plymouth since the war.'*

Before the principal speakers had their say John Foot reiterated the appeal for funds: *'We want money,'* he said bluntly. *'We want it to pay for the professional services and advice which we have received and must go on*

Above: *23 May 1957: The Earl of Mount Edgcumbe, John Betjeman, Lord Mayor Leslie Paul and AL Rowse on their way into the Prysten House for 'the most important public meeting in Plymouth since the war'. Right: New Street.*

receiving; we want it to buy properties; and, most of all, to restore them and make them habitable and useful buildings again.'

Dr Rowse, in his speech said: 'We must retain the Westcountry character of the place. I am all in favour of modern architecture, and the more modern the better. But when you get an entirely modern city, it might as well be anywhere – Plymouth, Birmingham or Cincinatti. We want to keep what preserves the historical flavour of Plymouth. We want to keep this not only for our own sake, but as guardians for people overseas who are generous to us. More and more people come to these islands, not to see what they have got in their country already, but to see what they would give their eyes to have – the Elizabethan buildings of this city.'

Following, John Betjeman, after he'd been found (he'd taken a detour via a Barbican hostelry where Walton Gale from the OPS had tracked him down, sharing a pint and some poems with the locals), said that *'until yesterday afternoon I had never made a really thorough investigation of the Barbican and had no idea how wonderful it was.'*

Winding up the proceedings, the Lord Mayor, who had presided over the meeting, said that he *'believed that the Society's proposals will have an important bearing upon the trade and the prosperity of the city.'*

John Macgregor's drawing showing how the same might appear, with later buildings cleared away - from the Old Plymouth Society appeal statement. May 1957.

Within days of the meeting it was announced that the fund had gone past the £1,000 mark but Stanley Edgcumbe, the Secretary of the Appeals Committee, thought that somewhere between £5,000 and £10,000 would be needed. Professor GM Trevelyan, the historian, and TS Eliot, the poet, also added their names to the list of patrons and John Betjeman wrote of the Society's *'imaginative and sensitive plan for the reconstruction of this historic little fishing port – the hidden heart of Plymouth'* in his City and Suburban column in the *Spectator*.

Meanwhile, a potential problem in the shape of street, widths raised itself. The Old Plymouth Society were determined that where old properties were demolished the street line at least should be preserved. However, under the bye-laws, the distance between the front of a house and that of the one opposite was supposed to be not less than 24 feet – *'and in New Street and the surrounding district, it is considerably less.'*

'The society are pointing out however, that if this section of the Act were acted upon by all local authorities most of the picturesque villages of Cornwall, such as Polperro, St Ives and Mevagissey, would have to be pulled down.'

When they next met, the Plymouth Housing Committee decided to recommend to the Council that the Old Plymouth Society's proposals be agreed. Furthermore having given the Society three months to come up with their plan, they now gave the body twelve months to submit proposals for the actual preservation of those buildings – that is at least those buildings the Corporation already owned – some of the buildings under consideration were not owned by the Council.

'The Housing Committee is recommending the Council to exercise its slum-clearance powers in respect of those which have been represented as being unfit by the Medical Officer of Health. It will be open for representations to be made for the preservation of Nos. 12, 15, 23, 31, and 44 in which the Society has declared an interest.' WMN

On Monday, 24 June, the full Council offered the Old Plymouth Society, through its non-profit making company, a 999-year lease on nine houses in New Street and Looe Street, at a fixed rent, on condition the offer was taken up within three months: *'Provision for the later consideration of other houses – one on the Barbican front, the others in New-street and Looe-street – is made in the Council decision.'*

It was a less fiery meeting than of late. Stanley Goodman thanked the Housing Committee for its *'consideration and reasonableness'* while Councillor Miller said that he hoped that the sincerity expressed would endure in the negotiations to come.

With the Barbican issue now, to a certain extent, resolved, the City Engineer and City Architect could begin work in Lambhay Hill and Castle Street. Meanwhile, Harold Pattinson managed to extract an encouraging statement from the Minister of Works, Hugh Molson, when he visited Plymouth in the first week of July; *'Having seen the Barbican today'* he said that he thought it would be *'appropriate to make an application for financial help for the preservation of historic buildings there,'* and, he added, *'I shall most certainly refer this to my advisory council.'* Molson, who had been appointed Minister earlier in the year, had previously been Parliamentary Secretary to the previous Minister from 1951-53, so he had a good idea what could and couldn't be achieved, although he did say that not all applications were granted

In August *The Times* reported on the Old Plymouth Society's progress and noted that the:

'Minister of Housing and Local Government had assured the Council that they need have no anxieties that the non-payment of slum clearance grants will be the price of failure to demolish all buildings in the proposed clearance areas, A condition that any houses retained should not be used as permanent habitations has not disturbed the society, for in recent weeks they have received applications for tenancies for reconditioned accommodation from clubs, youth organizations, artists in search of studios and other who want room for other business purposes, A sub-committee will asses the merits of the many claims.'

New Street, showing the 1930s flats at the top of Pin Lane.

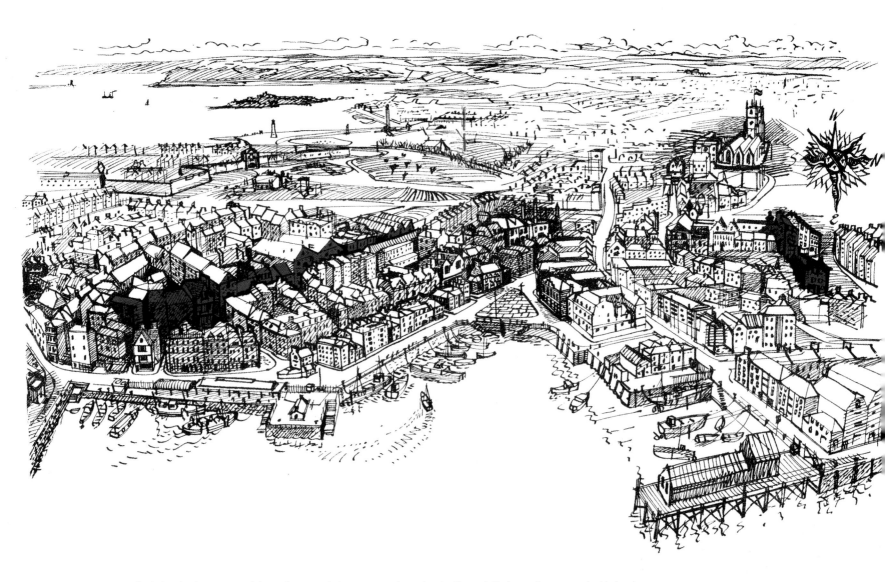

Geoff Clarke's bird's-eye view of the Batbican, with the properites leased to the Plymouth Barbican Association highlighted.

THE PLYMOUTH BARBICAN ASSOCIATION

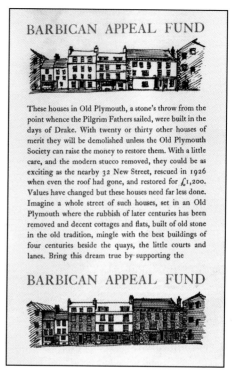

By October the financial details of the arrangement were becoming clearer, the Housing Committee were offering the newly-constituted Plymouth Barbican Association ground rents of £60 per annum for the New Street properties and £19 for the two Looe Street houses. The Plymouth Barbican Association, the new name of the company set up by the Old Plymouth Society sub-committee, would henceforth operate as a stand alone company limited by guarantee. Its objectives, as set out in its Memorandum and Articles of Association included:

'To take over the assets and liabilities of the unincorporated body known as the Old Plymouth Society Barbican Appeal Fund and to continue and develop the activities of that body.'

'To acquire land and buildings of historic or architectural value and interest in the City of Plymouth and to restore, preserve, improve, manage, develop, mortgage, lease or otherwise dispose of the same.'

'To undertake research into all questions in any way relating to the origin and history of lands and buildings in which the Association is interested either as owners or otherwise.'

'To develop public interest in all aspects of the records, history and construction of and relating to lands and buildings in Plymouth and to collect and distribute information of historical and constructional interest.'

'To produce, prepare, edit, publish, and distribute books, journals, pamphlets, articles and other publications dealing with the objects of the Association and either by itself or in co-operation with others to produce and exhibit cinematograph films dealing as aforesaid to assist in the preparation, organisation and giving of broadcast talks, discussions, lectures and tours.'

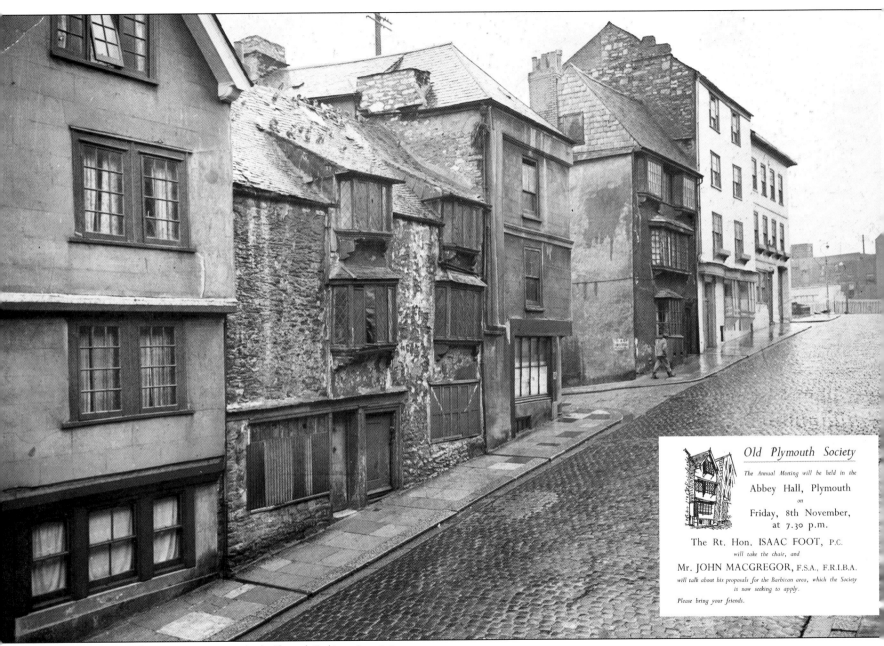

Looe Street prior to restoration by the Plymouth Barbican Association.

At the Old Plymouth Society AGM, on Friday, 8 November, 1957, the Chairman, Isaac Foot, announced that gifts totalling over £500 had been added to fund that very day, but that they were now looking to raise £50,000 to do the work they wanted to do. In a separate appeal document the Appeal Fund had attempted to set out the scale of costs involved;

'How much to restore a house? Probably to put one in perfect order, with indoor lavatories, and all modern conveniences, would cost £1,500 to £2,000, depending on the house. That includes all fees. To rip up the backyard and make a garden, another £200. To remove the stucco and re-point the stonework of the house, another £250.'

It was a lot of money to raise and even though the membership of the Old Plymouth Society had increased from 58 in May 1956 to 322 in October 1957, it was obvious that some of the funding was going to have to come from beyond the City boundaries. The appeal message was sent out far and wide, indeed the fifty daughter Plymouths scattered throughout the world, were all approached. Around Christmas time another Appeal Fund brochure was produced featuring sketches by Geoff Clarke, whose studio was in the heart of the Barbican.

'I do congratulate you on the beautiful leaflet,' wrote John Betjeman, while the secretary of the Society for the Protection of Ancient Buildings said she thought it was the best appeal the Society had received … *'if you care to let me have 1,500 to 2,000 copies I will see that they are circulated.'*

The *Western Independent* leader article joined in the appeal. *'The scheme must not be allowed to fail,'* wrote the eitor at the end of a stirring piece of prose. Meanwhile the assistant editor of the *Western Morning News*, Crispin Gill, was named in an advertising column of the paper as one of the first members of the council of the newly-formed Plymouth Barbican Association. Others included Jim Woodrow, Humphrey Woollcombe, Mr CP Brown, Gerald Whitmarsh, Edwin Masson Phillips, Stanley Edgcumbe, Peter Stedman, Hilary Cornish and the Rt Hon Earl of Mount Edgcumbe, the first four named bravely agreeing, at the insistence of the Council, to put up a guarantee of £25,000 (a massive sum at the time) chargeable against their estates, as a pledge that the scheme would be completed.

At the end of November it emerged that work on the Lambhay Hill area was set to start early in the new year; originally the Corporation planned

John Macgregor addresses the Old Plymouth Society in Abbey Hall.
Top: *Macgregor outlines his plans to Lady Astor, the Earl of Mount Edgcumbe and Isaac Foot.*

Above and opposite: *Stanley Edgcumbe and Jim Woodrow lead officals on a tour of New Street.*

to start with four cottages on the blitzed site of St Saviour's Church, but the Ministry of Housing had now agreed to seven.

'Some quaint narrow alleys and tiny courts will be retained by building across them on slender columns,' but the only buildings expected to be retained across the wider site were St Saviour's Hall and vicarage and the Fisherman's Arms. Exempted from the Compulsory Purchase Order that will eventually clear the Lambhay Hill area are the Seamen's Bethel, Cattewater Harbour Commissioners' offices and the Admiral McBride public-house.'

By March 1958 some £3,000 had been raised and four more properties had been added to the Plymouth Barbican Association portfolio: Nos. 12 and 23 New Street, No.6 the Barbican (alongside the Cattewater Harbour offices) and No.36 Looe Street. In June, three months ahead of their deadline, plans were submitted for the first nine properties. Alderman Pattinson, the Housing Chairman, said that the Association's proposals had met with the warm approval of the Committee, and those submitted for New Street were particularly interesting.

'The proposals reflect credit on the Plymouth Barbican Association who are undertaking substantial financial commitments in an endeavour to preserve the best of old Plymouth for posterity.'

As the summer came so did good news from the Central Government; the Minister of Works, Molson, appears to have been true to his promise. Stanley Edgcumbe, secretary of the Plymouth Barbican Association, received a letter to say: 'The Ministry of Works has now considered the recommendation of the Historic Buildings Committee for England on your application of a grant towards the cost of repairs to these buildings. Assuming the work can be done satisfactorily the Ministry is willing to make a grant.' The grants were for work on 37 and 38 New Street, and No.36 Looe Street. Mr Edgcumbe said that the Association now intended to apply for grants for work on six or seven other properties.

A few weeks later further glad tidings came in the shape of a £2,000 cheque from the Pilgrim Trust, an American philanthropic organisation, founded in 1930 by the late Edward S Harkness of New York who vested £2,000,000 in the hands of trustees *'for the benefit of Britain.'* The donation brought the total fund to nearly £8,000. *'Some doubting Thomases thought we would never even reach anything like £8,000. They thought the case was hopeless,'* beamed a happy Mr Edgcumbe.

As the Barbican Association were getting on with restoring their newly-acquired ancient buildings, so the Corporation were pressing ahead with their new flats. A suggestion that financial constraints may push the City Fathers into building Star flats (an off-the-shelf design already used in the area) for the Parade was met with antipathy at the Old Plymouth Society's July meeting, preference being expressed for the style of the new Woolster Street accommodation.

At the same meeting OPS Secretary Walton Gale showed a tablet which was to be erected in the preserved ruins of Charles Church as a memorial to the civilians of Plymouth who died in the last war.

Meanwhile, the fundraising went on apace. Concerts were staged and proceeds given over; lectures were delivered on the same basis and on Sunday 7 December 1958, the BBC gave the Association airtime to make an appeal as 'This Week's Good Cause'. The President of the Old Plymouth Society, a seasoned broadcaster, former MP and Lord Mayor of Plymouth, raised in Notte Street in the late-nineteenth century, Isaac Foot, gave the address.

'It is the intention to produce a book in which the names of all those who contribute to the fund will be recorded. As an old Barbican boy myself, my name will be in that book, I would like your names to be in it as well. It will be another Book of Plymouth,' he told listeners.

That same month another ambitious plan was unveiled for the Barbican area as local surveyor, D Gaskell Brown of Newton Ferrers gave the local papers his proposals for Plymouth becoming a Sailing Centre. With a yacht club on Fisher's Nose, from which ocean racing could start, a Sailing Club on Sutton Jetty and the removal of the Fish Quay to the other side of Sutton Pool, Mr Gaskell Brown felt that Barbican area could become the most popular and up-to-date yachting centre in the country.

Then, just before the year was out and on the eve of his retirement, the City Engineer, J Paton Watson, was pleasantly surprised to find that the first seven dwellings to replace *'the disgraceful slums'* on Lambhay Hill were to be called Paton Watson Quadrate. Alderman Pattinson, presiding, said that the new development was *'partly Mr Watson's own conception – in conjunction with the City Architect he has achieved something unique and outstanding.'*

The Lord Mayor, Alderman GJ Wingett, praised the City Engineer's use of

all sorts of materials - part of the Widey Court gates (the headquarters of the Royalists during the Civil War and recently pulled down along with the Widey Court itself) were incorporated in the new block.

No sooner had this block been opened than plans were released for a £67,000 scheme for the same style of properties, incorporating forty homes, in Castle Street. Although it was noted that *'the reluctance of people to move is hampering slum clearance plans on the Barbican and elsewhere'*: presumably these local folk were not part of the 96 - 97% of residents who, according to those who would have bulldozed the Barbican, were unhappy in their disgraceful hovels.

Top: *A distant view of Lambhay Hill and St Saviour's.* Bottom: *Lambhay Street flats.*
Opposite page: *Plymouth 1961; Note the big hole where High Street used to be.*

A NEW LEASE OF LIFE

n August 1959 work began on the restoration of No.36 Looe Street. Craftsmen from the firm of Dudley Coles restored the roof, replastered the walls, repaired floors and remade a fine copy of the original door (the original had gone to the Museum and had earlier been coveted by the Old Plymouth Society for 32 New Street, thirty years earlier).

Towards the end of February 1960 the building was ready: the first completely renovated old house in the Plymouth Barbican Association's portfolio. The cost? £3,000; half of which had been met by a grant from the Historic Buildings' Council. It was a red-letter day for the Association and for the Society that had spawned it: *'If it had not been for us – the Old Plymouth Society'*, said a very happy Stanley Edgcumbe, *'the house would undoubtedly have been demolished.'*

Above: The first building restored by the Plymouth Barbican Association - 36 Looe Street. Right: 4th June 1964, formal opening of the renovated 33 Looe Street with l-r: The Earl of Mount Edgcumbe, Lord Mayor Tom Watkins, Peter Stedman, Humphrey Woollcombe, Hilary Cornish, Stanley Edgcumbe, Arthur Marshman and Walton Gale.

The Looe Street property is, of course, in the same block as the Plymouth Arts Centre (which had been opened in October 1947 by Sir Kenneth Clark – prior to that it had most recently been part of the Virginia House development donated by the Astors) and it was fitting that this building on the bottom corner of the block should have been the scene of the first restoration, for it was in the Arts Centre, three years earlier, *'late one afternoon in February 1957 that a group of men and women met to see what could be done to save the ancient houses from slum-clearance.'*

'Apart from some members of the Old Plymouth Society, they had no organisation, no funds, no experience of such rescue work, and in many cases did not even know each other. The group decided to join the Old Plymouth Society, after all they had been formed in 1926 to fight a similar battle. Then they had bought and restored 32 New Street.'

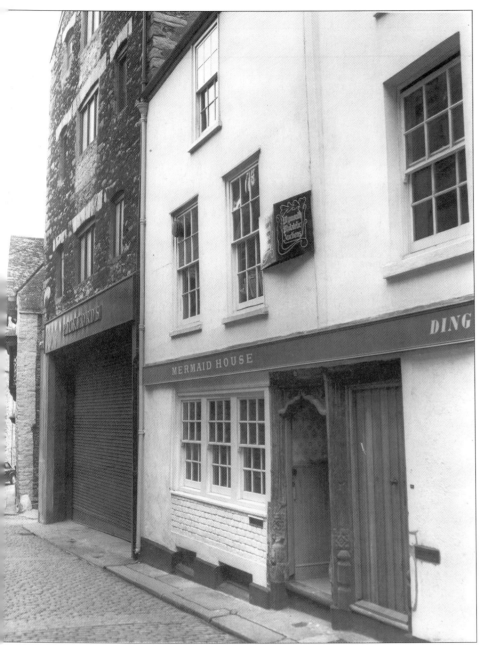

A stamp dealer moves into 34 New Street. Right; Southside Street is given a makeover.

'Since that early victory the Old Plymouth Society had very naturally become a little aged. With an influx of new blood and a battle to fight, the society was a giant refreshed.'

So wrote Crispin Gill, in a progress report printed verbatim in the *Western Morning News*, thus for the first time publicly identifying himself as the author of a piece about the whole saga. Reviewing the *'first two years'* work', he outlined the financial state of affairs, even after all the donations, the grants and rents had been received there was little left in the kitty now after this first completed job. With fourteen properties now to work on, and two in quite a derelict state, *'tremendous developments are only delayed by one thing – the unwillingness of people to reach into their pockets,'* he wrote.

By the end of 1961, with the help of grants from the Ministry of Works, via the Historic Buildings Council, the New Street properties had been restored and tenants had been found: *'A stamp dealer, a printer, an antique dealer, a maker of jewellery and a restorer of furniture were among the original tenants. A fine limestone warehouse in New Street was bought the following year and fitted out with a new roof and then turned into three flats.'*

'In partnership with the City Council the Association carried out an improvement scheme for Southside Street in 1961 with the encouragement of the Civic Trust. Street lighting was moved to brackets on the houses, the street furniture tidied and improved, and a painting scheme designed for the whole street carried out by the owner of the various properties. The development of a partnership between the City Council, the people living in the area and the Association, has been a major achievement,' wrote Gill in a later appraisal (1972) of the Association's work – *The Barbican Revived.*

Since that watershed moment in 1957 when the Plymouth Barbican Association was formed and the Council's remit regarding 'slum clearance' was clarified, the Barbican issue has been much less contentious. Planning has been more carefully scrutinised at every juncture, the Listed status of buildings has been altogether more effective through measures becoming more readily enforceable, not just locally but nationally, and the argument that so many informed, but seemingly outnumbered, voices raised about the Barbican area being an asset to the City historically and thereby commercially, has gained general acceptance. There are few Plymothians today who would not concede that the area, along with the Hoe, is the

brightest jewel in the City's crown. That this is the case is undoubtedly down to those who worked hard and tirelessly – and without remuneration – to create that august organisation, an organisation that still moves forward today on exactly the same basis.

After just ten years it was already clear that the Plymouth Barbican Association had not only proved the 'doubting Thomases' wrong, but had become a very successful body indeed, so much so that the guarantors were released from their liabilities. It was an achievement that put Plymouth at the forefront of the Conservation Movement nationally. In July 1971 the Civic Trust submitted a report to the Department of the Environment – 'Financing the Preservation of Old Buildings' – in which they mentioned twenty-two local building preservation trusts - Plymouth Barbican Association was the seventh largest. At the end of 1971 it owned just over 20 properties. In the detailed examinations of the various trusts more space was afforded to the Barbican Association than any other organization.

'The Plymouth Barbican project has been described in some detail as it is a good working example of an important preservation programme carried through with vision, courage, good management, and effective collaboration between a local preservation trust and the relevant departments of national and local government.'

In 1969-70 the delightful Elizabethan Gardens were laid out on the open spaces behind Nos. 34–40 New Street, between the warehouses. The space had been created by the removal of the crowded tenements that had been erected on the original Tudor and Jacobean gardens in the middle of the nineteenth century. Designed by Alan Miller Williams and incorporating numerous pieces of old Plymouth stonework rescued from the City Engineer's stores, the Gardens feature period planting, ornamental hedges, and pond. The gateway hard by the pond was originally sited, in 1630, in the entrance to the Hospital of the Poor's Portion in Catherine Street, next door to St Andrew's Church. Another feature is the sixteenth century doorway removed from the former Mayoral House in Woolster Street.

In 1971-72 the bombed block of properties at the back of the Island House – long an eyesore on account of its prominent position - was rebuilt. The Association owned one of the properties and sold it to a developer as long there was an understanding that they would be able to have a say in the appearance of the development. Also in 1972 the Pilgrim Trust advanced the Association £5,000 towards the purchase and

Left and far left: *the Elizabethan Gardens.*
Above: *the restored rear elevation of 34 New Street.*

conversion of 14 and 15 New Street – vital to the street line. That same year, after all the fuss about 'unfit buildings' the redbrick Railway Receiving Office building was converted into living accommodation.

Continuing to maintain and improve their properties, the Association re-roofed and repainted the New Street buildings. In the 1990s, the back of No.34 was uncovered and the original timber frame structure revealed and restored to its original condition, with the aid and encouragement of English Heritage.

'A detailed study of the architectural history of the house, rented since 1984 by Chris Robinson, showed how the original front had been tiered out over the street like the neighbouring 32. A proposal to restore it to this Elizabethan condition was opposed by English Heritage on the grounds that this would not be historically precise and that it was changing a nineteenth-century conversion. This was met with incredulity by the Association but they had to accept the authority of English Heritage (Gill: Barbican Revived 3rd Edition, 1995)'

And therein, in a strange way, lay the dilemma now facing the Association … what now was the way forward? A few years earlier they had looked at purchasing No.17 New Street, opposite the Elizabethan House. However, after carefully considering the matter they were able to stand back in the fairly safe knowledge that even if they didn't buy it the building would almost certainly be 'safe' because of the restrictions, through being Listed, that would be in place for anyone wishing to redevelop the premises.

The Planners, whoever they may be, both at Government and Local level were now obliged to be on the side of the Preservationists, provided that the building was deemed worthy enough. It was a far cry from the situation that had brought concerned members of the public together with members of the Old Plymouth Society, the Chamber and Junior Chamber almost forty years earlier. Happily, the collective consciousness had moved on and the story of the Historic Barbican since 1957 very much reflects that.

AFTER THE BATTLE FOR THE BARBICAN

Just as the Plymouth Barbican Association were tackling their first major restoration, so a number of other developments were unfolding. With their focus fully on their own new-found responsibilities, the former Old Plymouth Society offshoot largely left others to fight for those parts of the Barbican that were not in their portfolio and sadly, having to some extent lost their corner, the Corporation, still under the 'sweepers', picked off a number of choice old buildings that were in the way of proposed redevelopment. Admittedly some of these properties had gone in the fifties, like the ancient Spread Eagle on the corner of Kinterbury Street and Treville Street; the eighteenth-century Household of Faith Sunday School building (the first in the Three Towns) attached to Charles Church, the Charles Church vicarage - all these plus many other buildings that appeared in the Ministry of Local Government and Planning provisional list of buildings of architectural and historic interest, published in December 1949, and revised two years later.

Some, like the well-appointed row of properties laid out beyond Exeter Street in 1811 – Brunswick Terrace – went only after a brave fight by the Old Plymouth Society led by Stanley Goodman. The Society, however, were more successful, with regard to another, much older structure, in 1962, when they fought a long and bitter campaign to save Mount Batten Tower. Although by no means a Barbican building itself, it undoubtedly forms a significant part of the historic landscape of that area.

The Air Ministry, who had jurisdiction over what was then RAF Mount Batten, claimed that the expense of saving the tower was prohibitive – as the rocks that the seventeenth-century tower was standing on were unsafe. However, thanks to the OPS and the intervention of local MPs - most notably Sir Henry Studholme - the tower, built on the orders of Charles II at the same time as the Citadel, was saved.

Left: The ancient and soon-to-be-demolished Spread Eagle in Kinterbury Street. Above right: Of these buildings on the Parade only the Robert Crawford buildings, currently Harbour Sports, survived redevelopment in the 1960s.

Left: *43, 44 & 45 New Street.*
Right: *the Trattoria Capri, later the Acropolis Restaurant, built on the site of the old Mayflower Hotel, and since demolished.*

Meanwhile, inspired by the actions of the Plymouth Barbican Association, Dennis Browning, a local potter, and his wife, Mary, decided to purchase one of the buildings in New Street that the Association had not acquired, but which nevertheless had a demolition order on it – 44 New Street. That sale went through in 1962 and the following year the Brownings completed their purchase with 43 New Street. Shortly afterwards both buildings were reprieved and listed. With redbrick Queen Anne frontages, the buildings, which stand on part of the site of the old Greyfriars' Monastery at the bottom of Castle Dyke Lane, are thought to be extensions of two Elizabethan cottages which stood at right angles to New Street itself.

Clearly the perception of the Barbican held by some, including, a good number of active councillors, of it being a no-go slum area, was changing. Anyone prepared to invest in the area was welcomed and it seems that few eyebrows were raised when planning was approved for the typically sixties, low-slung restaurant, Trattoria Capri, when it appeared on the site of the blitzed Mayflower Hotel.

Equally clearly, the area's old-worldliness was attracting ever-increasing numbers of enlightened younger people – 'arty ne'er do-wells' as some would have them. The pub and restaurant scene started to take off in those swinging sixties. The blitzed Queen's Arms was rebuilt in 1966

as a much more sympathetically designed structure than the Trattoria. The following year the erstwhile Robin Hood pub, in New Street, was completely refurbished by the Barbican Association and opened as the Robin Hood Club, one of the city's first really late-night, night-clubs. Gaskell Brown, he of the ideas for Plymouth becoming a nationally respected sailing centre, opened the Sailing School night club off Vauxhall Quay. Meanwhile the Quay Club itself opened firstly on the jetty opposite and then moved up to the top of the building next door to the Custom House.

With all these changes taking place in the area, the City Fathers were happy to throw their corporate weight behind plans for celebrating the 350th Anniversary of the Sailing of the Pilgrim Fathers. As it transpired Mayflower '70 was a bit of a non event, but it did give the Plymouth Barbican Association the impetus to develop the Elizabethan Gardens and, in the absence of a replica *Mayflower* or *Golden Hind*, it did prompt the Maritime Trust to think that Sutton Harbour might be a good place to anchor the recently restored *Kathleen & May* as a tourist attraction. The ship was restored at Cremyll by Mashfords and one of the first visitors was the founder of the Maritime Trust, the Lord High Steward of Plymouth, the Duke of Edinburgh.

Sadly, visitor numbers appeared not to justify the decision and in 1978 she was moved to the then recently-restored Victorian Dock, St Catherine's in London. However, her temporary presence undoubtedly added to the uplifting effect that was gradually working its way around the waterfront and in 1975, following a trend that had started in London a few years earlier, two wine bars opened here, one in Southside Street, by John Dudley (later to be immortalized in another in another of his ventures as Cap'n Jasper), the other, overlooking the *Kathleen & May* in an old warehouse. Restored by local builder Richard Cross, who also did some fine work with the only buildings destined to survive in High Street (now called Buckwell Street), this hitherto unassuming warehouse became the Barbican Wine Lodge and further opened people's eyes to how any of the buildings in this historic area could be brought into play given the right treatment.

By this time the Local Authority had started to get the message themselves. Thanks greatly to the efforts of one man, Plymouth Museum

Left: Southside Street before and after the rebuilding of the bombed Queen's Arms
Right: The Kathleen and May, on the Barbican for most of the 1970s.

The restored Merchant's House and the innapropriately sited Magistrates' Court.

and Art Gallery Curator, James Barber, the splendid sixteenth-century merchant's house (much embellished in the seventeenth century) in St Andrew Street was restored by the City Council over a five-year period and opened to the public as a mini Plymouth museum in 1977.

Not all the old buildings that were redeveloped were as obvious as No. 33 St Andrew Street, however, In 1980, the erstwhile Coroner's Court, a nineteenth-century building off what had been Tin Street, became a clothing store, while a year or two later, Isaac Foot senior's old Christian Mission Hall, in Notte Street, became a restaurant. Around the same time Jack Nash (another Foot relative) refashioned warehouse space between Southside Street and the Parade to form 'The House that Jack Built' a multi-unit shopping complex populated by small and very independent retailers – with accommodation on the top floors.

It became a familiar pattern, old warehouses were found to be very adaptable spaces, not just as antique centres. Former schoolmaster David King took on warehouse properties on the Parade and Vauxhall Quay and timber merchant Richard Hills tackled Palace Vaults in New Street. Further up New Street, and opposite the Barbican Association's properties, the much-praised (within the industry at least) Hanover Court housing development was created. With a series of angled corners abutting the street, the architects were congratulated for maintaining the street-line and yet allowing more light into the flats. Further up the street again the next great warehouse, in 1988, became the short-lived home of the Armada Experience, an interesting visitor-experience that was ultimately blown out of the water by the Corporation's own visitor attraction that opened the following year – Plymouth Dome on the Hoe.

As a visitor attraction the Dome was undoubtedly better situated and it lasted longer but, after years of being underfunded by the Local Authority, it was eventually closed in 2006. In the meantime, however, the Council had opened another attraction, the Mayflower Visitor Centre. This was built on the site of the Trattoria Capri, already mentioned as being built in the sixties on the bombed site of the earlier Mayflower Hotel. Demonstrating spectacularly that they had little idea of what visitors to the Barbican actually wanted to see at the beginning of the twenty-first century, this attraction closed with almost indecent haste after about three months. Today, the badly-designed building (functionally and aesthetically) is home to the Tourist Information Office on the ground floor while the original displays limp on upstairs for the benefit of those either unaware of how awful it is or simply looking for shelter.

Just as so many of the Council members failed to understand why the Barbican was worth preserving in the first place, so their successors consistently fail to appreciate what it is people want to see and do when they do come here. The story of the Merchant's House is typical of that lack of understanding.

No sooner had the City finished the five years of careful restoration of No. 33 St Andrew Street than the planners immediately shot themselves in the foot by allowing the Magistrates' Court to be built between this wonderful old building and St Andrew's Church itself. While the court building itself is undoubtedly one of the better post-war pieces of architecture, its location could hardly have been more offensive. The streets radiating out from the town's mother church are inevitably going to be the oldest streets in the area and, as such, an absolutely key ingredient of the Historic Quarter. It is no great leap of reasoning to suggest that if Plymouth was, after all, going to try to make a real feature of its unique heritage that the ancient street pattern would be a major ingredient in its success or otherwise. Sadly, however, there has been a marked failure to understand that idea, or at least to act upon it.

Consequently it is not only the St Andrew street access to the harbour that has been built across – not withstanding the difficult-to-traverse pedestrian area to the east of the court building – but the Whimple Street access too has been radically redesigned.

Time was when Whimple Street ran straight into High Street and then across into Looe Street. The junction of these thoroughfares was the principal junction of the Elizabethan town. Here it was that the old town cross was placed; here the town crier, in the days before modern communications and even newspapers or broadsheets, would read proclamations and inform the citizens; here it was that the town's first

St Andrew Street, before and after it was severed in two by the Magistrates' Court.

Whimple Street before the War when it was a major hub of the old town, and now a backwater.

purpose-built Guildhall was erected in 1606, and here, some 350 years later the Corporation erected a Labour Exchange and allowed an electricity sub-station to be placed.

The long-familiar triangular site was gone – and for what reason? After the Jacobean Guildhall, the site had housed its Georgian replacement and that building stood until the final year of the War, gutted, but capable of restoration had anyone risen to the challenge. Certainly it's a shame that something didn't happen here to retain the old street pattern, for this route, even in its restricted form, is still a principal pathway to the old part of Plymouth from the City Centre.

What divides the Historic Quarter even more effectively from the City Centre, however, is the refashioned Notte Street and Vauxhall Street which, together, in pratice make the old area north of this route a less colourful and less interesting adjunct to the Barbican, whereas in reality this is the truly old part and what we celebrate today as the heart of old Plymouth is principally the Elizabethan extension to Plymouth writ large.

Looe Street is much older, as were, in their day, St Andrew Street, Finewell Street, How Street, Buckwell Street, Kinterbury Street, High Street, Breton Side, Bilbury Street, Exeter Street, Foxhole Street and Woolster Street (the latter two both now subsumed within the modern Vauxhall Street).

High Street suffered serious losses after the 'Battle for the Barbican' had been 'resolved' and curtailing its bottom end so that Vauxhall Street could be widened seriously altered the old street pattern, despite vague lip service being paid the old thoroughfare (there is an area under the flats at the bottom of what is now called Buckwell Street which is supposed to extend the roadway visually if not actually.

If only the much-talked-about Northern Relief Road could be created to take through-traffic away from the Barbican altogether, then and only then could the old part of Plymouth begin to function in the way it should, as an homogenous and predominantly pedestrian historic precinct.

Until that time it will always be a split site, the bottom half of which is markedly more pretty than the top. Of course, part of the reason for this is the way the Corporation planned their housing here - their blocks of flats built in the fifties and sixties without any of the promised community centres or shops. With How Street on one side and the equally sterile Stillman Street on the other, Looe Street, despite being blessed with the Arts Centre, the Minerva (the oldest building to house a pub in the area), the Porter's Arms and a couple of other commercial properties, somehow lacks the colour of the Parade or Southside Street, as, to a lesser extent does New Street, despite its attractions including the Elizabethan House, Elizabethan Gardens and a number of other interesting and ancient properties.

The Barbican area generally, taking in both sides of the Vauxhall Street divide, encompasses the largest single area of cobbled street surfaces in the country and yet it still lacks the critical mixed use of buildings that would make the whole area much more successful. The sort of balance required is that first pioneered around the Parade as one by one empty warehouses, or warehouses used for business, were redeveloped above first floor level for housing, leaving ground-floor potential for shops, cafés, bars and restaurants.

See the Parade today when the sun shines and the outdoor seating areas beneath the giant umbrellas (installed by the Sutton Harbour Company) and you are looking at one of the most attractive tourist honeypots in the country. It is a formula that the Sutton Harbour Company, and other developers, have taken to duplicating around the perimeters of the Pool, each development tending to become a little more ambitious, some say greedy, in terms of the number of floors/apartments they build above their downstairs eateries.

Here again is an issue that threatens the area today, not clearing slums to build flats, but clearing perfectly good buildings to build much bigger ones with everyone clamouring to have a sea view. In 1990 the architecturally acclaimed Co-op warehouse, built just 30 years earlier, was demolished, making way, a decade later, for an apartment block (Discovery Wharf). The proposal was, unsuccessfully, opposed by Sutton Harbour and its subsequent realisation, along with that of Mariner's Court, effectively kick started the upwardly mobile refashioning, as opposed to conversion, of the Sutton Harbour waterfront.

One of the City Centre's greatest features is the fact that it substantially represents one distinct period of architecture and with it a very strict ruling on building height. It would be a disaster for the character of the shopping centre if, within that Old Town Street/Mayflower Street/Market Street/Royal Parade perimeter, the height restriction was to be severely compromised. Similarly, part of the great charm of the Barbican is that few structures within the heart of the Historic Precinct stand markedly taller than the others and it would be a tragedy and a travesty if such structures were

North Quay, with the 1960s Co-op warehouse - Above - and today with new developments.

Looking out over West Pier, before and after; the lock gates were installed; the Fish Market moved to the old Coal Wharf site and the National Marine Aquarium was built at Teat's Hill.

allowed to infiltrate the area. Already the northern and eastern borders of the harbour have gone down that path, but happily a recent proposal to build up and over Vauxhall Quay was turned down.

The Sutton Harbour Company, the statutory harbour authority owning and controlling Sutton Harbour, has done a fantastic job of transforming both the appearance and the economic viability of the area in recent years. It owns all the quays and roadways around the Harbour and a number of the old buildings: the old Fish Market, China House, etc. as well as the freehold of the Harbour. It was also behind the award-winnning eight-storey Pinnacle Quay building. Current proposals, include plans (drawn up in partnership with Plymouth City Council and the Mackay Design Panel) for an eleven-story accomodation scheme between Pinnacle Quay and the nine-floor, ten-storey East Quay House.

'It will fill in one of the last missing links in creating a circular walk around the harbour and will be a vital part of the wider aspiration to link the East End to the waterfront,' said current Sutton Harbour Managing Director, Nigel Godefroy.

The installation of lock gates (to which the public have access but make no contribution towards), the inexorable spread of moorings, the removal of the Fish Market to the other side of the harbour, the building of the National Marine Aquarium and the infilling of Lockyer's Quay have all been part of Sutton Harbour's ongoing modernisation process that has been happening over hundreds of years, and which accounts for there being properties in the wider Barbican area from every one of the last eight centuries, but let's not forget how that came to pass or how it is that those older buildings still survive. Let's hope just that the developers don't end up shooting themselves in the foot by overdeveloping the more historic, western part of the Harbour's waterfront that all these new developments look out over.

As well as all of Sutton Harbour's major developments, the 1990s witnessed one or two smaller but, in their way, very significant and sensitive projects in the Barbican area. One, in New Street, was a new-build. After years of neglect, the few remaining properties opposite the Barbican Association's 34-40 block were pulled down and Cooper Construction, under David Colwill (who, in one capacity or another, has worked on Barbican Association properties since the beginning and who would later chair the Association) built John Sparke House, a sympathetic modern development that blends well with its surroundings (as indeed does Brock House at the bottom of Batter Street).

Quay Road after its most recent 'pedestrianisation'.

The other was on the other side of the harbour and is one of only a handful of warehouses left in the country to have seawater lapping on three of its four sides. Dating from the middle of the seventeenth century, this is the China House, and its million-pound-plus refurbishment as a large pub/restaurant represented a substantial leap of faith on behalf of Bass Breweries. It also marked the beginning of the invasion of the Barbican by the chain gangs.

In more recent years Wetherspoons, Subway and the Edinburgh Woollen Mill have all infiltrated the area, driving up rents and putting pressure on the independent retailers, restaurateurs and pub/club owners. One is reminded of Gordon Cullen's warning the City Fathers about the Shopping Centre: 'As the chain stores come in so the cream of the local society must emigrate and the vitality of the town is correspondingly reduced ...'

Fifty years ago Cullen, along with the rest of the world, saw the Barbican as an area threatened with demolition. Thanks to the valiant efforts of a number of people and, at the end of the day, most significantly the Plymouth Barbican Association, for they were the ones that turned talk into action, the Barbican was substantially saved, but I'm sure Gordon Cullen, who died in 1994, would be horrified to think his warning on the Shopping Centre now needed to be extended to that area that he thought, if preserved, 'could be a rallying point for all those who want to arrest the devitalization of provincial England.'

The West End of the City Centre is currently being promoted as Plymouth's Independent Quarter, but it too has been greatly compromised by the chain gangs. Back in the late 1980s, however, the Barbican, apart from one or two tied pubs, was completely free of the high-street chain operator, not so any more and the threat represented is a very real one. The Barbican retailers have already suffered one massive blow when the general introduction of Sunday Trading removed the area's unique advantage that it enjoyed in that respect by virtue of being a designated tourist area.

Of course, the other great irony in all this is the other slow but sure process whereby the Barbican Association is now positively being encouraged by the City Fathers to let some of those saved properties - properties that their predecessors condemned as 'hovels' and 'unfit for human habitation' - be used as living accommodation.

Overall, however, the future for the buildings themselves, whatever their usage, looks markedly more promising that it did fifty years ago. The

Opposite page: *The Barbican waterfront has changed enormously in the last ten years. Meanwhile, as we see above, the nineteenth-century Regent Inn (now the Swallow) is in danger of being swallowed up in the new high rise developments around Exeter Street*

Plymouth Barbican Association is still going strong, and, at the time of writing, still has one original member from 1957, Peter Stedman, on the board. There is also now a Barbican Businesses' Association, it succeeds the Barbican Traders' Group and the Barbican Traders' Association before that. For many years there was too, a Barbican Group, a monitoring body run by the tireless Stanley Goodman, who also was to keep the Old Plymouth Society alive through the comparatively quiet years of the 1970s and 1980s. Here and there there are residents groups too from the various accommodation centres scattered around the harbour. And there are, from time to time, special Local Authority groups and panels set up to deal with Barbican issues.

Thus it is. with little likelihood of the area being in imminent danger, we can look to pass the historic baton on to the next generation. But just remember how much was so nearly lost, and indeed how much was lost, and not just to the enemy from airfields across the Channel but to the enemy within, both before and after the War – despite their protestations that they were acting for the benefit of the people; people who for the most part did indeed want to be helped - but not relocated.

Part of the old victualling yard on Commercial Wharf, cleared in the 1930s

Buildings deemed to be of Historic Interest in the Barbican Area:

Arthur Southcombe Parker Snr. first compiled his Civic Survey of the antiquarian buildings of Old Plymouth in the closing years of the First World War. It was a remarkable undertaking, making full use of his knowledge of architectural history, his drawing skills and, it would appear, his social skills, for it seems that he was able to gain admission to almost any building he deemed to be of interest.

Pre-dating any nationally recognised means of 'listing' any significant parts of our architectural heritage, Southcombe Parker singled out two main categories of building he deemed most worthy of preservation: these he marked D - 'desirable' and VD - 'very desirable'. Today we have three gradations of listing Grades I, II* and II (superceding an earlier I, II and III format), with a fourth category - PC - indicating that any building or fabric thus described makes a 'Postive Contribution' to the area it sits within.

Clearly, in the 90 years that have elapsed since Parker's Survey, our view on what is worthy of any of these accolades has changed, after all, what was modern for Parker is now likely to be more than a century old; even so there are bound to be differences of opinion and on one page there appear a selection of those buildings around the Barbican which so far have escaped official recognition, and which the author hopes may, sooner rather than later, be included.

Meanwhile, what follows these pages is a tabulated version of the first forays into assessing the merits of the Old Plymouth's architectural heritage. Between them the first six surveys cover that period of the twentieth century during which local and national government really began to wake up to the idea of preserving the best of our heritage and then skips to the present day state of affairs - one where, thankfully, there is a healthy respect for the importance and the value, both in historic and financial terms, of conservation.

Sources:

1918 *A.S. Parker Civic Survey: Antiquarian Survey of Old Plymouth.*

1928 *Parker and Bracken. Ancient Buildings Survey for the newly-formed Old Plymouth Society.*

1943 *Parker, Masson-Phillips, Copeland and Bracken. Present State of the Ancient Buildings of Plymouth Nov-Dec 1942*

1947 *OS map with Location of Buildings of Architectural or Historic Interest*

1951 *Provisional List of Buildings of Architectural or Historic Interest for consideration in Connection with the Provisions of Section 30 of the Town and Country Planning Act, 1947. Revised August 1951.*

1958 *The Ancient Buildings of Plymouth, Copeland and Masson-Phillips for the Old Plymouth Society, 3rd Edition.*

2007 *Current Listing Status of Buildings in the Barbican area.*

Key:

Medieval = *Pre-1500*
Elizabethan = *Late-1500s*
Jacobean = *Early-1600s*
William and Mary = *Late-1600s*
Queen Anne = *Early-1700s*
Georgian = *1700s and very early 1800s*
C16 = *Sixteenth Century* C17 = *Seventeenth Century,* etc.
y = *building mentioned*
D = *Desirable in preservation terms.*
VD = *Very desirable in preservation terms.*
pc = *not listed but judged to make a Positive Contribution to the area*
III, II, II*, I = *Grade Three, Two, Two-star, One listing*
a = *Destroyed in the War*
b = *Badly damaged during the War.*
c = *Damaged.*
d = *Building intact*
u = *Gutted by fire in War, fate uncertain.*
ab = *Demolished before the War.*

BARBICAN AREA		1918	1929	1938	1942	1947	1951	1958	2007
COOKSLEY'S COURT	C19		y	y	y	y			
CAMBER'S COURT	1760-80		y	y	y	y			
MARTIN'S COURT	1860-70				y	y			
CASTLE STREET	Castle remains					II			II
12	1680 pole staircase	VD	y		y	y	y		
NEW STREET									
1	Early C19 warehouse								II
2	Early C19 warehouse								II
3	Early C19 warehouse								II
4 & 5	Early C19 warehouse	D							II
10	C18				u				
11	C18 red brick						III		
12	Late-C18				b	y			II
15	Early-C19. warehouse								II
26	Wm & Mary destroyed by fire pre-1939	VD	y	y	ab				
28	Wm & Mary destroyed by fire pre-1939	VD	y	p	ab				
30	c 1700	VD	y	y	c	III			
32	Elizabethan	VD	y	y	y	III	y	y	II*
33	1809					III			II
16	Elizabethan								II
18	Elizabethan	VD	y	y	y	II	II	y	II* sam
19	Early-C19 warehouse								II
22	Early C19 warehouse								II
24-25	C17 house remodelled C18/19								II
23/24	bollards/steps early-C19								II
27	Late-C18 warehouses								II
31	Early-C19 townhouse					III	III		II
34	Jacobean		y	y	y	II	II	y	II*
35	Jacobean		y	y	y	III	III	y	II
36	Jacobean		y	y	y	III	II	y	II*
37	C17 merchant's house		y	y	y	II	II	y	II
38	C17 merchant's house		y	y	y	II	II	y	II

BARBICAN AREA		1918	1929	1938	1942	1947	1951	1958	2007
39	C17 townhouse					III	III		II
40	C17 townhouse				y	III	III	y	II
41-42	Early-C18 warehouse						III		II
43	Queen Anne					III	III	y	II
44	Queen Anne			y		III	III	y	II
45	Queen Anne	D	y	y	y	III	III	y	II
45a	Queen Anne	D	y			III	III	y	II
47	1806 warehouses								II
TEAT'S HILL	Ivy Cottage 17th			y	y		III	y	
BARBICAN									
6	Late-C18								II
9	Late-C16 Island house	VD	y	y	c	II	II	y	II
	Watch House pulled down 1930s		y		ab				
	Emmigration Depot demolished1930s		y		a				
12	Georgian	VD	y	y	y	II	II	y	II
13	Georgian townhouse						III		II
14	Georgian public house Dolphin				y		y	y	II
	Two K6 telephone kiosks 1930s								II
STOKE'S LANE									
1	Early-C19								pc
7	Early-C19								pc
SOUTHSIDE STREET									
1 & 2	Demolished early-1960s						III		
5 & 6	Mid-C19 warehouse								II
10	Georgian townhouse								II
12						III			
15 to 18	Late-C19 retail and domestic								pc
20	Queen Anne	D	y	y	y	III	III	y	II
21	Queen Anne	D	y	y	y	III	III	y	II
22	Queen Anne	D	y	y	y	III	III	y	II
23	Queen Anne	D		y	y	III	III	y	II
24	Queen Anne	D		y	y	III	III	y	II
25 & 26	Mid-C19								

BARBICAN AREA		1918	1929	1938	1942	1947	1951	1958	2007
27 & 28	C19								pc
29 to 32	c1890s retail and domestic								pc
34	Late-C18 Navy Hotel			y	y		y	y	ll
35 to 37	Late-C19								pc
38	Elizabethan bakery								ll
39	Early-C19								ll
40	C-19								pc
41	C-18 - bombed				a				
43	Early-C19 shops								ll
44	Early-C19 shops								ll
45	Early-C19 shops								ll
45a	Early-C19 shops								ll
46 to 50	1898 retail and residential								pc
51	Jacobean sea captain's house	VD	y	y	y	ll	ll	y	ll
52	Georgian	D	y	y	y	ll	ll	y	ll
53	c1680 wine merchant's house	VD	y	y	c	ll	ll	y	ll
53a	c1680 wine merchant's house	VD				ll	ll	y	ll
54	c 1680	D	y	y	b	ll	ll	y	ll
55	c1600 Queen's Arms, bombed new build		y	y	a				pc (rebuild)
58	C18 bombed	D	y		a				
60	Part Medieval	VD	y	y	y	ll	ll	y	ll*
61	Part Medieval	VD	y	y	b	ll	ll	y	ll*
62	War damage not rebuilt	D		y	b				
63	Destroyed in war	D		y	a				
FRIARS LANE									
3	Georgian Trinity House			y	b	ll	ll	y	ll
	Collier's Wine Store 1765				y		y	y	
QUAY ROAD									
1	C18 Ship Inn				y	y	y	y	ll
7	Late-C18 warehouse								ll
8 to 9	Mid-C19 warehouse								ll
THE PARADE									
7	C19								ll

BARBICAN AREA		1918	1929	1938	1942	1947	1951	1958	2007
9	1847 warehouse								II
	Early-C17 Three Crowns								II
15	C18 Barbican Gallery								II
16	Early-C19								II
23	C17 or C18				y	III	III	y	
24	C17 townhouse	D	y	y	y	III	III	y	II
10	Custom House 1820			y	y	II	II	y	II*
18	Elizabethan Custom House	VD	y	y	b	II	II	y	II*
3	C18 Damaged in War		y	p	b	y			
4	C18 Queen's Arms. Demolished 1960s	D	y		y	II	III	y	
5 & 6	C17. Demolished early-1960s				y	II	III	y	
8 (19 Batter Street)	Queen Anne	VD	y	y	b	III	III		
11	C19 warehouse								pc
25	C19								pc
BATTER STREET									
19	Queen Anne. Demolished 1960s.				y	y	y	y	
LOWER BATTER ST									
24	c1600. Demolished 1950s.		y			y			
EXCHANGE STREET									
1	Jacobean Destroyed in War				a				
2	Jacobean Destroyed in War				a				
3	Early-C17 rear of Three Crowns				y		y	y	
WOOLSTER ST									
14	The Exchange early-C19 Destroyed in War.			y	a				
15-17	Good limestone front. Demolished c1959.					y	y	y	
20	Has C17 doorway. Removed post-war.			p	y	y	y	y	
41	c1720. Destroyed in War.				a				
42	c1740. Destroyed in War.		y	p	a				
31	Ring o Bells 1580, pulled down 1956	VD	y	y	y	II	y	II	
CATHERINE STREET									
The Dispensary	Built 1798				y		y	y	II
	Synagogue 1762								II*
	Abbey Hall late-C19								II

BARBICAN AREA		1918	1929	1938	1942	1947	1951	1958	2007
FINEWELL STREET									
7	*C18. Destroyed in War.*				a				
8	*C18 Destroyed in War*				a				
10	*Early-C18. Destroyed in War.*				a				
	C15 Prysten House. Tanners Restaurant		y		c		l	y	l
PALACE STREET	*St Theresa's (Thomas's?)*						.		pc
	Palace Court annex								pc
45	*Late-C18 New Inn Demolished early-1960s*							y	
HIGH STREET									
44	*c1600. Pole staircase. Demolished 1937.*		y		ab				
48	*Early C17. Demolished 1937.*	D	y		ab				
45	*Early C17. Demolished 1937.*		y		ab				
46	*Nichols Ct. Elizabethan. Demolished. 1937*		y		ab				
49	*C17 Demolished 1937*	D			ab				
50	*Queen Anne front. Demolished 1937.*		y		ab				
52	*C17. Demolished 1937.*	D	y		ab				
53	*Queen Anne. Demolished 1937.*	D	y		ab				
54	*Queen Anne. Demolished 1937.*	D	y		ab				
55	*Queen Anne. Demolished 1937.*		y		ab				
20	*C17 Naval Reserve Inn*		y		y	y	y		
22 & 23	*Queen Anne. Destroyed before 1939.*	VD	y		ab				
24	*C18. Demolished early-1960s*	D			y	y	y	y	
17	*Part Elizabethan. Demolished c1960.*	D	y	y	y	y	III	y	
18	*Demolished c1960.*	VD			y	y	III	y	
19	*Demolished c1960.*	VD			y	y	III	y	
1	*C18 front Destroyed in War*			y	a				
2 & 3	*Old house. Destroyed in War, pole stair*				a				
4	*1400-1500 carcase. Destroyed in War.*		y	y	a				
5	*Elizabethan. Destroyed in War.*	VD	y	y	a				
8	*Elizabethan. Destroyed before 1939.*		y		ab				
63	*Ancient structure. Front removed after War.*						y	y	
12 Buckwell St (64 High St)	*Elizabethan*		y		y		y	y	ll
18 Buckwell St (61 High St)									pc

BARBICAN AREA		1918	1929	1938	1942	1947	1951	1958	2007
HIGHER LANE									
	Artic House								pc
6									pc
PRINCESS STREET									
19	*C18*						y		
PRINCESS PLACE (Notte Street)									
1 - 6	*Early-mid-C19. Demolished 1960s.*						III		
NOTTE STREET									
2, 3, 4	*Demolished 1950s.*							III	
6	*Golden Fleece. Destroyed in War*		y	y	a				
7	*c1650. Destroyed in War*	VD	y	y	a				
12	*C17 Rebuilt 1883. Demolished c1960*	VD	y	y	y	y	II	y	
13 & 14	*Queen Anne. Destroyed in War*	D	y	y	a				
58	*Mission Hall 1883*		y	y	u	y	III	y	pc
ST ANDREW ST									
1	*Mid-C19*								II
2	*Mid-C19*								II
2	*Mid-C19*								II
3	*Mid-C19*								II
4	*Mid-C19*								II
5	*1860s*								II
16 to 18	*C19*								pc
27	*Jacobean or earlier. Demolished post-1958*				y	y	y	y	
33	*Elizabethan. The Merchant's House*	VD	y	c		y	II	y	II*
34	*Elizabethan. Demolished 1930s.*	VD	y	ab					
ST ANDREW'S CHURCH	*Gutted during War, rebuilt 1950s.*								I
GUILDHALL/OLD TREASURY	*Gutted during War, rebulit 1950s*								II
LOOE STREET									
1 to 9	*1898 Municiapl Housing*								II
16-20	*1898 Municipal Housing*								II
40	*Virginia House entrance*								II
38	*C18 townhouse Plymouth Arts Centre*	D			y	III	III	y	II
37	*C18 incl Tudor elements*				y	II	II	y	II

BARBICAN AREA		1918	1929	1938	1942	1947	1951	1958	2007
36	Jacobean	VD	y	y	y	II	II	y	II*
35 (1 Batter Street)	C17 Painter's Arms Demolished 1960s				y	III	IIIy	y	
33	c1560s, oriel windows	VD	y		y	II	II	y	
30	C18					III	III		II
31	C16 Minerva, pole staircase	D	y	y	y	II	III	y	II
32	Late-C16 with pole straircase	D	y	y	y	II	II	y	II
22	c1600. Demolished 1930s.	D	y	y	ab				
25	Late-C18				y	y	III	y	pc
26	Adams mantlepiece		y	p	y	y	y	y	
27	Early-C18				y	III	III	y	II
28	Mid-C19					III	III		II
29	c1700	D	y		y	III	III	y	II
VAUXHALL ST									
2 (now 94)	c1740	D	y	y	y	III	III		II
4	c1670	VD	y	y	y	III	III		
5	Brick warehouserf inscribed 1804				c		III		
6	c1695, destroyed in War.	VD	y	y	a				
3	C16 Prince George Inn Demolished c1959	VD	y		b	III	III		
1	C17 Steam Packet Inn Demolished c1959	VD	y		b	III	III		
54	Early C19 warehouse								II
56	Early C19 warehouse, Monsen's								II
62	C19 warehouse								pc
82 to 84	Mid-late-C19 warehouses								II
115-131	1898 Municipal housing								II
134									pc
140	Former C19 mortuary								II
155	Former Royal Exchange Inn								pc
VAUXHALL QUAY	Early-mid-C19 Monsen's Warehouse								II
	Early-C19 store, now bar.								II
BRETONSIDE									
2 to 4	s								pc
35 to 47	C19 shop								pc
36	Former 1930s cinema								pc

BARBICAN AREA		1918	1929	1938	1942	1947	1951	1958	2007
44									pc
51 & 53	*C19 Friary Hotel*								pc
50 TO 54	*C20 rebuild on site of 1655 house.*								ll
	Treville Street School								pc
	Martin's Gate						lll	y	pc
WHIMPLE STREET									
6	*C18. Demolished c1960.*			p	y	y	y	y	
7 to 10									pc
11	*Mid-C19 commercial premises*								ll
27	*C17. Destroyed in War.*				a				
35	*Elizabethan. Destroyed in War.*		y	p	a				
34	*Elizabethan. Destroyed in War.*		y	p	a				
40	*c1796. Destroyed in War.*				a				
41	*c1786. Destroyed in War.*				a				
	1800 Guildhall. Gutted during War.				u				
KINTERBURY ST									
7	*c1600. Destroyed in War.*	D	y	y	a				
32	*c1700. Demolished 1930s.*	D	y		ab				
33	*c1700. Demolished 1930s.*	D	y		ab				
28	*early Georgian. Destroyed in War.*		y		a				
BUCKWELL LANE	*Wesleyan Chapel b1792. Destroyed in War.*								
BUCKWELL STREET	*Grantie archway*								ll
7	*C18. Destroyed in War.*				a				
8	*C18. Destroyed in War.*				a				
22	*C18. Demolished 1930s.*				ab				
23	*C18. Demolished 1930s.*				ab				
26	*C18. Demolished 1930s.*				ab				
Devon Inn	*Destroyed in War.*				a				
TREVILLE STREET									
30 - 31	*Late-C17 pole stair. Destroyed in War.*				a				
46 (now 21/23 Bretonside)	*c1630 King's Head*		y	p	y		y	y	ll
50	*c1690. Destroyed in War.*	VD	y		a				

BARBICAN AREA		1918	1929	1938	1942	1947	1951	1958	2007
51	c1690. Destroyed in War.	VD	y		a				
59	C17 timber fronted. Demolished in 1938.				ab				
71	c1787. Destroyed in War.				a				
EXETER STREET									
1	C17. Demolished post-war.		y	p	y				
2	C17 Demolished post-war.		y	p	y				
3	C17. Demolished post-war.		y	p	y				
15	c1700	D							
129	c1635 rebuilt 1939ish		y	p	rebuilt		III	y	
130	C17. Demolished 1930s.		y		ab				
131	C18. Demolished 1930s.		y		ab				
101	c1809 with older parts. Demolished 1930s				ab				
HILL STREET									
2	C18. Demolished 1960s				y		II	y	
3	C18. Demolished 1960s				y		II	y	
4	C18. Demolished 1960s				y		II	y	
5	C18. Demolished 1960s				y		y	y	
6	C18. Demolished 1960s				y		y	y	
7	c1600. Demolished 1930s.		y	p	ab				
8	c1600. Demolished 1930s.		y	p	ab				
9	c1600. Demolished 1930s.				ab				
MOON STREET									
16	Queen Anne. Demolished 1930s.		y		ab				
NORTH STREET									
1	Queen Anne. Demolished 1930s.		y		ab				
2	C18. Demolished 1930s		y		ab				
3	C18. Demolished 1930s		y		ab				
13	Late-C18				y		y		
14	Late-C17. Demolished 1930s				ab				
15	C18t. Slate-hung. Demolished 1930s				ab				
The Clinic	C18 house				y		y		
39 - 43	Early-C19							y	
66	c1600. Demolished 1930s		y		ab				

BARBICAN AREA		1918	1929	1938	1942	1947	1951	1958	2007
71	C17. Pole staircase. Demolished 1930s		y		ab				
72	Queen Anne. Demolished 1930s		y		ab				
GASKING STREET									
Corner House	c1780		y						
BRUNSWICK TERR									
1 - 9	c1790. Demolished 1960s.		y	y	c		II		
NORLEY STREET	Charles Church						I		
6 Charles Vicarage	c1650. Demolished 1950s.		y	y	b				
7	Georgian. Demolished 1950s.	VD			y		y but		
MORLEY STREET									
7	Georgian. Demolished 1950s.		y	y					
VENNEL STREET	C18 Household of Faith. Demolished c1959.		y	y	y				
4		D							
GREEN STREET									
Corporation Almshouses	Rebuilt C19 orig 1679				y u		y		
HEWER'S ROW	C18 houses. Demolished 1937.				ab		y		
1 - 4	Late-C18						III		
GASCOYNE STREET									
6	c1780. Destroyed in War.				a				
7	c1780. Destroyed in War.				a				
8	c1780. Badly damaged in War.				b				
9	C18				y		y		
10	C18				y		y		
11	Woodside Tavern				y		y		
REGENT STREET									
11	Early C19						III	y	
PARK STREET all houses	Built 1809. Demolished by 1960s.						y		
HOE STREET									
12	Late C17. Redeveloped 1950s.				y				
13	Late-C17 Redeveloped 1950s.				y				
15 & 16	c1782			y	y		III		
24	C19 townhouse								pc
Hoegate House	C19								pc

BARBICAN AREA		1918	1929	1938	1942	1947	1951	1958	2007
HOEGATE STREET									
	Warehouse behind Distillery								pc
1	*Warehouse, datestone 1746*			p	a				
2	*Warehouse datestone 1769*			p	a				
7a									pc
LOWER STREET									
9	*Late-C17*				ab				
HIGHER STREET									
12	*Late-C18*				b				
EBRINGTON STREET	*C18 Hampton House*								
Mayflower Sailing Club	*Early-C19*								||
West Pier	*Late-C18*								||
Sutton Harbour Quay	*Late-C18 and C19*								||
HOE GARDENS									
1 - 4	*Mid-C19*						III		||
5 - 8	*Mid-C19*						III		||
Hoe Garden House	*Mid-C19. Buried under new road.*						III		
STILLMAN STREET									
29	*C19*							y	
40 - 41	*Early-C19 house and store*								||
SUTTON WHARF	*Warehouse*								||
5	*Warehouse*								||
HOW STREET									
1 to 15	*Late-C19 municipal housing*								||
16 to 21	*Late-C19 municipal housing*								||
	Offices								pc
CITADEL ROAD 217-315	*C19 houses*								pc
LAMBHAY HILL	*Late-C19 St Saviour's Hall*								pc

CTORIAL GUIDE TO THE HISTORIC BUILDINGS OF THE BARBICAN

Commercial Inn
Lambhay Hill, late-C19

Fisherman's Arms
Lambhay Street C18

Admiral MacBride
Barbican, late-C18

Cattewater Harbour Commission
Barbican, C19

Barbican Theatre
Former seaman's bethel, 1885

...lotte Inn
...lotte Street, C19

Sutton Wharf/Vauxhall Street
1930s flats

The Cooperage
c1804 Vauxhall Street

Vauxhall Street Warehouse
Dated 1892

Breton Side
Former Co-operative store, erected 1903.

Breton Side
C19 Regent Inn - The Swallow...

NB None of the selection on this page are currently listed or deemed to make a particular contribution to the area.

Mayflower Sailing Club, Phoenix Wharf: Grade II
Early C19 former warehouse, included for its historical and group value.

West Pier, Barbican: Grade II
Origins in C17, but mainly 1791-99 when it was one of two facing piers built across the old Cawsey, the entrance to the Harbour. Contains various plaques and memorials including the 1933 Mayflower Memorial.

Castle Remains, Lambhay Street: SAM 217 Grade II
Although subject of some dispute, the listing suggests that these are the remains of the 'South Port' of the Medieval (C14 or C15) castle that gives Plymouth its civic crest.

Sutton Harbour Quay: Grade II
The Quay running around Northern and Western perimeter of the Harbour from North East Quay to West Pier. Late C18 and C19, includes Vauxhall Quay and the Whitehouse Pier.

6 The Barbican: Grade II

Thought to be late C18 and used as 'South Western Receiving Office for Goods and Parcels' in C19. **PBA**

9 'Island House': Grade II

Late C16 or early C17 (it may have been damaged by fire and rebuilt) it retains many original features.

12 The Barbican: Grade II

Mid-late C18, painted brick with tall staircase window at the back.

13 The Barbican: Grade II

Late C18 town house, rendered brick facade, with late C19 shop front.

Dolphin Hotel: Grade II

Early C19 pub - core possibly earlier - Tolpuddle Martyrs stayed here in March 1838. Stone floor on ground level.

Two Telephone Kiosks: Grade II

K6 type kiosks designed in 1935 by Sir Giles Gilbert Scott. Cast iron.

The Old Fish Market: Grade II

Built 1896 to designs of Sir James Inglis, engineer of the Great Western Railway. Adapted by Form Design for Sutton Harbour for retail use after removal of Fish Market to the other side of the Harbour 100 years later.

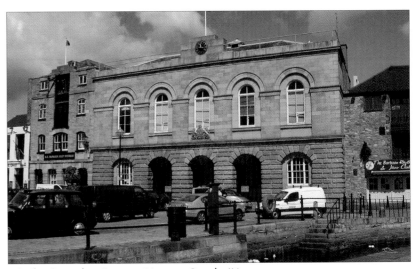

7 The Parade: Grade II
Listed largely for side wall which incoporates wall of C17 house into 3-storey early C19 warehouse.

9 The Parade: Grade II
Monsen's Ship Stores - 1847 datestone, Plymouth limestone dressings.

10 The Parade, Custom House: Grade II*
Built by Mr Ball and designed by David Laing it superceded the old Custom House on 1st January 1820. The clock was added in 1823. Bonded stores behind extend building into Vauxhall Street.

11 The Parade: PC
Old warehouse - valued but not listed.

Three Crowns: Grade II
Thought to be early C17 with later mid-C19 remodelling it predates the neighbouring warehouse and Custom House.

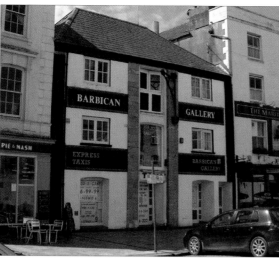

15 The Parade: Grade II
Mid-C19 shop on corner of Parade Ope.

Warehouse: Grade II
Probably C18 converted to art gallery late C20.

16 Maritime: Grade II
Early C19 shop knocked through to form second frontage of the Martime Inn, late C20.

18 The Parade, Old Custom House: Grade II*
C16 former merchant's house, bears inscription 'A 1623 K' over right-hand doorway, possibly used as Barracks (hence Parade) saved by Old Plymouth Society 1926, gutted during WWII - rebuilt.

24 The Parade: Grade II
C18 town house with possible earlier core, refashioned as The House That Jack Built c1980.

25 The Parade: PC
Where artist Robert Lenkiewicz created his library.
PBA

1-4 New Street: Grade II
Large, early-C19 warehouse converted to living accommodation 1990s.

12 New Street, The Robin Hood: Grade II
Late-C18, licensed premises from at least 1798. **PBA**

15 New Street: Grade II
Early C19 warehouse included for contribution to street. Ground floor gallery, late C20 flats above.

16 New Street: Grade II
Early C20 warehouse on eastern corner of White Lane.

17 New Street: Grade II*
Late-C16 or early-C17 merchant's house with fine timber-frame frontage. Now Liberty shop with flat above.

18 New Street: Grade II
Early C19 warehouse on site of C17 building (with surviving fireplace).

22 New Street: Grade II
Early-C19 warehouse incorporating wall of earlier building, now flats. **PBA**

Bollards/Steps in front of 23/24 New Street: Grade II
Probably early C19.

24/5 New Street: Grade II
C17 house remodelled in C18 and C19. Now shop and house with many early features.

27 New Street: Grade II
Late-C18, early-C19 set of warehouses built around a courtyard approached via carriageway ope. Antiques centre.

31 New Street: Grade II
Early-C19 townhouse, probably a remodelling of a much earlier property - currently a restaurant.

32 New Street: Grade II*
Known as the Elizabethan House Museum, but possibly Jacobean, saved by the OPS in 1926. Open April-October.

33 New Street: Grade II
Palace Vaults - has datestone 1809 and was built to house Napoleonic War booty.

34 New Street: Grade II*
Jacobean timber-frame house, remodelled front C19. Original pole staircase and carved doorway. Author's studio since 1984. **PBA**

35 New Street: Grade II
Jacobean merchant's or sea captain's house, one of pair with No.34. **PBA**

36 New Street: Grade II
C17 merchant's house with remodelled front elevation. Good C17 panelling and staircase. **PBA**

37 New Street: Grade II
C17 merchant's house one of pair with No.38. Pole staircase and other early features. **PBA**

38 New Street: Grade II
C17 merchant's house one of pair (37). Pole staircase and other early features. **PBA**

39 & 40 New Street: Grade II
C17 townhouse. later refashioned as two dwellings. Front rebuilt C18. 39 has fine C18 staircase. 40 has some C18 panelling & studwork. **PBA**

41/42 New Street: Grade II
Warehouses c1800 converted to apartments 2006. **PBA**

43 & 44 New Street: Grade II
Early C18 townhouses thought to be built on core of two C16 properties which stood at right angles to New Street and on site of medieval Greyfriars Monastery.

45 & 45a New Street: Grade II
C18 town house, extended C19, painted brick front.

47 New Street: Grade II
Pair of warehouses, recently converted for apartments. Datestone insbribed 'I.C.1806'

t Saviour's Church: PC
ate-C19

217-235 Citadel Road East: PC
C19

5 & 6 Southside Street: Grade II
Mid-C19 Plymouth limestone warehouses currently in use as Pannier Market.

10 Southside Street: Grade II
Late-C18 town house with later shop, now part of The House That Jack Built.

15 to 18 Southside Street: PC
Late-C19 Shops and houses..

20-21 Southside Street: Grade II
-C18 Plymouth limestone rubble town houses with later shops.

22 Southside Street: Grade II
Early-C18 townhouse, painted brick with later windows.

23 & 24 Southside Street: Grade II
Large, early-C18 town house, single-depth, original plan much altered by insertion of tall shop-front, now restaurant.

25 & 26 Southside Street: Grade II *Mid-C19 property, Yarmouth Stores Ltd. outfitters, have been based in 25 since late-C19.*

27 & 28 Southside Street: PC *C19*

29-32 Southside Street: PC *C1890s Shops and accommodation.*

33-33a Southside Street: Grade II *Early-mid C19 shop and house with later shop (includes 12 Quay Road. Now restaurant.*

No.34 Southside Street: Grade II *Late-C18 Navy Hotel, render on brick with later windows.*

No. 35 & 37 Southside Street: PC .

38 Southside Street: Grade II *Late-C16 bakery still trading..*

39 Southside Street: Grade II *Early-C19 front, earlier core.*

40 Southside Street: PC *C19.*

43-45a Southside Street: Grade II
Terrace of three early-19C shops with accommodation above.

46-50 Southside Street: Grade II
1898 shops with accommodation above.

51 Southside Street: Grade II
Early-17C merchant's/sea captain's house. Timber frame with original moulded doorway. Building restored in the 1930s.

52 Southside Street: Grade II
Mid-C18 with earlier core.

53 Southside Street: Grade II *C17 wine merchant's house with C18 alrerations.*

54 Southside Street: Grade II *C17 refashioned in C18.*
.

3 Friars Lane: Grade II
Mid-C18 town house, Trinity House now offices.
.

55 Southside Street: PC
1960s public house on site of bombed C16 hostelry.

162

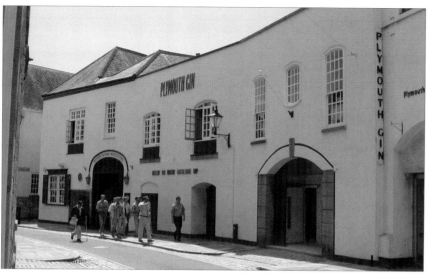

Hoegate Street: PC
Warehouse backing on to Gin Distillery.

60 & 61 Southside Street: Grade II*
Gin Distillery since late-C18; building dates back to C16 and appears to incorporate elements of neighbouring medieval Greyfriars Monastery. Impressive refectory area.

24 Hoe Street: PC
Large C19 townhouse - Margaret Macmillan nursery school since 1935.

Hoegate House: PC
C19 town house.

1-4 Hoe Gardens: Grade II
Mid-C19 mews terrace with walls, steps and railings.

5-8 Hoe Gardens: Grade II
Mid-C19 mews terrace with walls steps and railings.

7a Hoegate Street: PC

1 Looe Street: Grade II
Part of 1898 local authority development.

1-15 Looe Street: Grade II
Part of 1898 municipal development, significant for being first local authority housing scheme in the area.

16-22 Looe Street: Grade II
Part of 1898 municipal development, significant for being first loca authority housing scheme in the area.

25 Looe Street: PC

27 Looe Street: Grade II
Mid-C18 townhouse with later shop.

28 Looe Street: G II
Mid-C19 townhouse with shop and earlier core.

29 Looe Street: G II
C18 townhouse with shop. **PBA**

30 Looe Street: Grade II
C18 or early-C19 remodelling c earlier townhouse.

31 Looe Street: Grade II
Late-C16 townhouse long since adapted as Minerva public house, pole staircase, original panelling and many period features.

32 Looe Street: Grade II
Late C16 townhouse with pole staircase, home of Barbican Association SW Image Bank.

33 Looe Street: Grade II
C17 merchant's house, restored and rebuilt in C20. **PBA**

Batter Street Chapel: Grade II
Plymouth's first nonconformist chapel c1702, part of the Astor development since 1923.

36 Looe Street: Grade II
Early-C17 townhouse, timber-frame and rubble. **PBA**

37 Looe Street: Grade II
Shop with accommodation, good period shopfront - c1800.

38 Looe Street: Grade II
Early-mid-C18 townhouse with later shop, Plymouth Arts Centre since 1940s.

54 & 56 Vauxhall Street: Grade II
Early-C19 warehouses, formerly 49 & 50 Woolster Street - 54 incorporates No.5 Barbican Court.

62 Vauxhall Street: PC
C19 warehouse.

82-84 Vauxhall Street: Grade II
Two pairs of mid-late–C19 warehouses, Plymouth limestone rubble.

94 Vauxhall Street: Grade II
Early C19 building includes warehouse facing onto Vauxhall Quay and integral counting house.

Vauxhall Quay: Grade II
Monsen's warehouse aka Breton House, early-mid-C19 converted to flats 1970s.

Vauxhall Quay: Grade II
Early-C19 store, converted to bar late 1990s.

115-131 Vauxhall Street: Grade II
Opened on 5 December 1898, terrace of local authority housing designed by James Paton, Borough Engineer and Architect.

155 Vauxhall Street: PC
Former Royal Exchange Inn

140 Vauxhall Street: Grade II
Late-C19 mortuary (closed 1970s) since used a shop. Plymouth limestone.

1-15 How Street: Grade II
1898 terrace of local authority housing, part of practically complete block of council flats.

16-21 How Street: Grade II
1898 terrace of local authority housing, part of practically complete block of council flats, with corner shop.

Offices How Street: PC

50-54 Bretonside: Grade II
C20 substantial rebuild of 1655 property.

44 Bretonside: PC

51-53 Bretonside: PC
C19 Friary Hotel on site of earlier Black Bull.

35-47 Bretonside: PC

36 Bretonside: PC
1930s former Plaza Cinema.

King's Head Bretonside: Grade II
Early C17, beam in bar inscribed 1629, oldest public house in continuous use on the Barbican

Martin's Gate & Treville Street Board School: PC

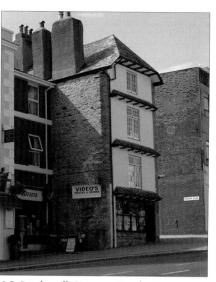

18 Buckwell Street: PC
One of the few ancient survivors in Plymouth's High Street.

12 Buckwell Street: Grade II
Late-C17 with restored front, formerly in High Street.

No.s 7-10 Whimple Street: PC
.

11 Whimple Street: Grade II
Mid-C19 commercial premises.

1-3 St Andrew Street: Grade II
Mid-C19 commercial development..

4 St Andrew Street: GII *Mid-C19 shop with accommodation.*

5 St Andrew Street: Grade II
1860s Abbey Hotel built on site of medieval Turk's Head, currently Kitty O'Hanlons.

Plymouth Guilhdall: Grade II
Built 1870-74 deisgined by Norman and Hine, includes City Treasury building at rear. Reduced to a shell during the Blitz it was reconstructed, with a number of changes and after much consideration, in the late-1950s.

Civic Centre: Grade II
Opened by Queen Elizabeth II in 1962 the complex was designed by City Architect HJW Stirling in the early-1950s and modified and completed by Jellicoe and Ballantyne 1957-62.

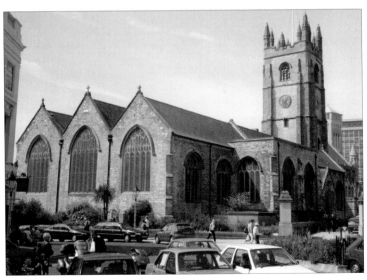

St Andrew's Church: Grade I
Tower and much of the main fabric date from C15 but there has been a church on this site since C10. Completely gutted during the Blitz it was subsequently rebuilt in the 1950s and reconsecrated in 1957. Stained glass windows (E&W) by John Piper 1958.

Abbey Hall: Grade II
Church Hall and Assembly rooms 1890s, adjacent to St Andrew's Church in Catherine Street and abutting 'Prysten House'.

Dispensary: Grade II
Slate-hung at rear, Plymouth limestone ashlar front. 1807-09 with inscribed date of 1798, date of foundation of the Public Dispensary. A significant and early example of this building type.

Synagogue: Grade II*
Oldest Ashkenazi Synagogue in the English-speaking world in continuous use. Built in 1762 interior little changed with most original wood and brass features. Extended slightly on centenary in 1862.

Merchant's House: Grade II*
Home to several Mayors of Plymouth in C18 and to James Parker (Mayor 1608) property is thought to be mid-C15, remodelled late-C16 and further in C17. Restored by Plymouth City Council 1972-77 since when it has served as a local extension to the Plymouth Museum services.

Prysten House: Grade I *Excellent example of large late medieval (C15) merchant's house built on courtyard plan for Thomas Yogge, who died in 1509 and who part-funded construction of St Andrew's Church tower. Currently Tanner's Restaurant ground floor.*

Higher Lane: PC

St Theresa's Mission Church: PC

Palace Court Annexe: PC

Granite Archway: Grade II
Resited, C16 archway.

Virginia House Settlement: Grade II

40 Stillman Street: Grade II
*Early C19 house and store with many
original features, including Mid-C19
earth closet and washhouse with copper
in rear courtyard.*

58 & 59 Notte Street: PC
*Christian Mission Hall built by Isaac
Foot snr. 1880s. Converted as
restaurant since early 1980s.*

8&9 Quay Road: Grade II
Mid-C19 four-storey warehouse, Plymouth limestone rubble.

7 Quay Road: Grade II
Late-C18 Plymouth limestone waterside warehouse, now Cider Press public house.

3&4 Quay Road: Grade II
Former waterside warehouse, probably late-C18 with adjacent public house (formerly the Ship Inn) now all incorporated into one large public house.

No.1 Stoke's Lane: PC

No.7 Stoke's Lane: PC

No.5 Sutton Wharf: Grade II
C19 Plymouth limestone warehouse, one of least altered in Barbican area.

Sutton Wharf: Grade II
Plymouth limestone rubble warehouse with stone inscribed 'W.S. 1842'.

Index

High Street houses lost during the Wwar.